Victorian Furniture

Our American Heritage

By Kathryn McNerney

COLLECTOR BOOKS
A Division of Schroeder Publishing Co., Inc.

The current values of this book should be used only as a guide. They are not intended to set prices, which vary from one section of the country to another. Auction prices as well as dealer prices vary and are affected by condition as well as demand. Neither the Author nor the Publisher assumes responsibility for any losses that might be incurred as a result of consulting this guide.

Printed by IMAGE GRAPHICS, INC., Paducah, Kentucky

For
Sharon and Molly
Dotty and Mimi

Photography
Tom McNerney

Cover
Victorian Walnut Secretary.
Courtesy of
Choates Antique Shop
1623 Broadway, Paducah, KY 42001

Appreciation

A grateful thank you to everyone not only patient with the time it took to photograph but who expressed friendly interest by offering material that helped make this reference possible. (These permanent Malls and larger exhibiting Shows represent hundreds of dealers carrying furniture from most states.)

Riverfront Antiques ....Selma, AL.
Florida Sunshine shows,
    Cdr. Bill Faessel, Mgr. ....Gulf Coast Cites, FL.
Greater Pensacola Antique Dealers
    Ass'n Shows.......................................Pensacola, FL.
Magnolia Manor ....Cairo, IL.
Red Coach Antiques ....Teutopolis , IL.
Wm. G. Neptune Antiques ....Brooklyn, IN.
John & Debra Renschler ....Centerville, IN.
Vernon Webb's Auctions ....Centerville, IN.
P. Michels Jones Studio ....Crawfordsville, IN.
Arvin & Helen Grace's Antiques ....Evansville, IN.
Raxchel's Antiques Mall........................Evansville, IN.
Beauchamp's Den of Antiquity..............Indianapolis, IN.
Cox's Golden Rule Shop and
    Hoosier Antiques Exposition ....Indianapolis, IN.
Kinnett's Antiques..............................Martinsville, IN.
The Epleys ....Plainfield, IN.
Concord Antique Shop ....Concord, KY
Everett & Helen Livingston...................Gilbertsville, KY.
The Newtons.....................................Gilbertsville, KY
Joe Ley ....Louisville, KY.
Rex Lyons Antique Shows ....Louisville, KY.
Agnes McDaniels ....Murray, KY.
Courthouse Square Antiques......................Murray, KY.
Mavis Moore ....Murray, KY.
Walker's Antique Shop ....Paducah, KY.
Russellville Antique Mall ....Russellville, KY.
Hermitage Hall.....................Hermitage (Nashville), TN.
Blair's Antiques...............................Murfreesboro, TN.
Murfreesboro Antique Mall ....Murfreesboro, TN.
The Estate Gallery ....Murfreesboro, TN.
Marie Norris ....Smyrna, TN.

Contents

Introduction

To better understand the complexities of Victorian Furniture is to be aware of its rarely close relationship with the people of those days. Most often flashing into our minds at the word "Victorians" are The Romantics living in a curiously make-believe world. Ambitious enough to reject reality displeasing to them, inventive enough to bring forth and apply their own practical innovations that so radically improved our furniture universe, the Victorians were still too prudishly hesitant to flout rigid traditions and gossip by suddenly launching bold new ideas in the products themselves. For a long time they leaned, instead, with nostalgic dependency on past grandeurs, even into the medieval, thereby satisfying a longing for luxuries denied them through the ages, only gradually introducing basic changes.

As a mirror returns an image, so in this fashion did the furniture reflect rather than create the moods of the individuals, extending, enlarging, diminishing, enhancing (for Victorians decorated just about everything), even combining works of periods' predecessors. But their touches finally won a singular niche in our history.

In 1837 Britain's young Victoria began her reign. Soon on both sides of the Atlantic (on this side neatly packaged from an elastic 1840 to a firmer 1900) the years became Victoriana, the products Victorian, and the people Victorians.

We cannot, however, automatically so-describe as typical everything made nor each person. Among the endless parade of Lovelies was a heap of junk. Gingerbread trims adored in the cities found among deliberated acceptance their fussiness tone down to simpler country/frontier needs. Even with steadily evolving land and water transportation, when bulky items too cumbersome to ship from factories or unable to be sent in the local knockdown manner for destination reassembling were locally copied, things too often differed from patterns sent by manufacturers. Sharing in the era but not typically of its aggrandized affluence, were the plainer but no less appealing wares (Pie Safes, Jelly Cupboards, etc.) of the Shakers, Zoars, Scandinavians and the sturdy Palatinate feeling with the Pennsylvania Dutch, each producing in its geographical settlement. There were also the trailblazers opening up our western territories into vital new markets. Many who paused to strike it rich built fantastic Victoriana in mountain boom towns and along the Pacific coast, particularly in San Francisco. (The latter's five million dollar Palace Hotel in 1870 contained the finest Victorian furniture ever seen anywhere. In February 1876 friends honored one of the Silver Kings with a Palace dinner, guests seated on richly upholstered armchairs at a massively carved table, where menus had been engraved on solid silver plates made from ore mined at Nevada's Comstock Lode. And in remote rough mining regions whose towering peaks would ordinarily have made cartage unthinkable, Wells Fargo and narrow gauge railroads even hauled in grand pianos.) Others grubbed along for several generations in bleak prairie soddies. Everyone could not afford to be typically Victorian.

Acquisition

Land was the main source of power through the 1700's, the rich owning it, the poor working it. Tentative mass production and a shadowy middle class already struggling for precarious footholds emerged into full light at 1800, gathering amazing impetus by the 1850's. Farm laborers actually swamped towns exploding into cities, where undreamed-of wages brought modest advantages to some, true wealth to others. Mass production became our so-called Industrial Revolution, whereby luxuries soon were staples, made possible by steam driven machines as planing, band and jig saws, and lathe turners, along with the 1820 coiled spring advancing upholstering. Sections as table legs were rapidly made from a squared piece of wood inserted in a lathe, and while the lathe turned, a chisel handpressed against the wood cut the design; slower had been the earlier turnings from water-power and foot treadles. Skilled cabinetmakers owned large sets of varied size woodchisels. Shakers had been trying out the circular saw in light experimentation, but it now was seriously applied to finely cut veneers at tricky widths and thicknesses. Jig saws more easily made intricate fretwork (carpenter's lace).

Realizing its potential, previous woodmasters as far back as Adams and Chippendale had tried infant production methods. But it wasn't until 1830 that Lambert Hitchcock, having converted his Connecticut workshop into a factory around 1820, after several difficult attempts, successfully built a stable mass production, shipping then-expensive chair parts country-wide in large quantities. This meant that one group cut frames from ash, maple, and hickory; another cut rails; others painted a basic red and top coats of black, mustard yellow, or blues for colorful cost saving finish stencils of eagles, lyres, fruits, and flowers; finally, the original label was stenciled L. HITCHCOCK, HITCHCOCKSVILLE, CONN. WARRANTED, which has had subsequent changes. Production continues today in Riverton, Conn. (Hitchcocksville) with chairs being marked under their seat fronts. (Earliest fancy chairs often had scenic paintings on the splats. Hitchcock rockers might seem to combine Windsor lines.) Seats first of woven rushes became solid wood, later caned. Up to a hundred workers turned out many chairs a day while a single craftsman given the same hours doing the whole job himself from raw wood to finish might manage one. Other such fancy chairs unmarked are Hitchcock types. However, Jule Chalk in 1850–70 Ohio, one of several manufacturers who followed Hitchcock, branded his underside chair seats with an iron mallet. Kriemer & Bros. in 1873 Cincinnati, Ohio employed 300 workmen while that city's Mitchell & Rammelsberg in 1859 flourished at making similar chair designs (along with most cabinets). Records show that from the start to 1860 there were over 500 listed producers. Our furniture was not only being slowly but radically altered, now significant social changes occurred; in fact, American Victorians and their furniture tastes were under way!

If one word expressed the criterion of Victoriana it would have been MONEY. When Society admitted an impressionable Nouveau Riche (newly rich, Victorians doting on French phrases,) into its ranks, neither man nor his ancestry mattered much, only what he could spend in keeping up. The humblest clerk and tradesman saved until he could move his family into a 'suitable house in an eminently respectable' neighborhood, a haven whose walls shut out competitive business worries and nagging social insecurities. For regardless of the extent of his fortunes, and despite knowing he had pulled himself up by his own bootstraps, he needed crammed full rooms of overpowering shinbarkers as constant reassurance to prop up his underlying unease in such an atmosphere...and just as importantly...to impress others.

Victorians had money to spend. They wanted goods with almost unseemly haste and were willing to pay for it. Things could not possibly be handcrafted fast enough so manufacturers complied with rapidly-built factories, windows stuffed with enticements, and warerooms stacked to their ceilings. And whether they specialized in one or all categories, they sold in wholesale lots. People could choose from a remarkable assemblage of perplexing styles.

For patient buyers there were still many excellent cabinetmakers with regular and custom lines. Not until the 1870's was factory furniture plentiful enough to supply the general public nor more economically produced than in various cabinet shops. And in those years skilled craftsmen still made the finest deeply carved draperies, scrolls, tassels, etc., uncertain production cuttings often shallow and applied moldings flat and unsubstantial. Upon receiving an order, it was not unusual for a cabinetmaker to measure the room space for which an item was intended, and then if a forest was closeby, choose the very tree whose wood he planned to use. Those who had always owned their shops did not suddenly disappear in a puff of smoke. But it was awfully hard to maintain their normally high standards and reach necessary production goals for continuing competition with steadily improving factory methods and their convenient home mail and catalog business. Many craftsmen beyond river basins as the Ohio, Missouri, and Mississippi survived longer than shopowners farther east. But when a large general percentage could no longer hold on they went to the factories. Determined to be independent, some carried on by adopting a second enterprise. In New Orleans in 1868 French immigrants Pierre Abadie and A. Dubrille advertised to sell or repair furniture. Thomas Goddard of Newport, Rhode Island family cabinetmaking fame was also a repairer until 1858. In that same period Maine's Mark Fenderson made uncommonly exquisite carvings while Johann Ullman of Washington County, Texas achieved superb metropolitan detailed carvings seldom reached by rural masters making Cottage Furniture. George H. Monday, an 1835 Philadelphia Carver & Gilder, supplied mirror and picture frames in his own warerooms, meantime gilding chairs for manufacturers. It was not unusual that architects such as Charles & Henry Greene of California ably combined their first career with cabinetmaking, the Greenes' artifacts having Japanese and Mission as well as architectural shadings. In his Boston shops from 1845 until well into the 1860's, A. Eliers, a craftsman working in Louis XV substyle, also expertly built graceful freehanging (flying) staircases, shipping them as parts to mansions anywhere in the United States for local installations under his supervision. Too, his advertising emphasized that his was the only form in the country able to supply "at a moments notice" all furnishings to equip the interiors of homes, hotels, churches, and the like.

Architect John Hall in 1840 Baltimore published our first American book on furniture design, *The Cabinetmakers Assistant*. His own creations made quite an impact on Victorians, being first an absolute deluge of massive pieces in mahogany, then rosewood veneers on poplar or pine, heavily embellished. Baltimore Funeral Directors, Henry Jenkins & Son, added cabinetmaking to funeral duties in 1861. Theirs was a sober but short-lived effort at Elizabethan Revival since they had no real conception of that 1558–1603 Queen's preferences and ended up with purely colony versions. However, the practice of funeral directors retailing furniture did continue far into the 20th century, especially in smaller towns. William March Tweed, born into a cabinetmaking family of Scottish descent, served his apprenticeship, going on to make fine quality chairs and meeting house benches. He wholesaled "in the wood" – construction completed but without final painting, varnishing, caning, or upholstering. At the height of his career he left woodworking for politics, thereafter best remembered as New York City's "Boss Tweed."

On receipt of his catalog stated prices, one Philadelphia manufacturer offered to ship to any part of the world. And as from time immemorial, another enterprising Thinker operated his CHEAP FURNITURE STORE for secondhand merchandise in the late 1860's on Chicago's State Street.

With Boston and New York City still leading in furniture production Jamestown, N.Y. was one of the first communities in the Great Lakes area to pioneer the industry, growing rapidly from 1840 into the 1880's. First settled as an Indian fur trading post in 1836, Grand Rapids Michigan, was firmly established by 1850 as one of our principal manufacturing centers, and was considered the capital by 1870. They opened that year a semi-annual exhibition market which today remains active. Its large variety of mass produced inexpensive styles adaptations, especially Renaissance an Louis XVI Revivals, we call "Grand Rapids Furniture." Its makers quickly multiplied. Representative among them were Berkley & Gay, Nelson – Matter Co. with an 1876 catalog for export markets, August Behrens in 1890, the 1856 Geo. Pullman Company, Grand Rapids Chair Co. in 1892, and Hampton & Sons making upholstered sets 1850–1880. Most of the important furnishing houses were referred to as "Upholsterers." Skilled woodworkers emigrating from our eastern coasts, a great many Scots and Nordics were hired. The Scots with an outstanding homeland background in superlative ships' carvings easily transferred to furniture decorating. Fine carvers among the Italian immigrants were also sought, for although machine decorations were swift, the results were rough, and the hands of clever craftsman were still needed to refine them. Most skilled quality was very good, inferior workmanship not always stemming from unskilled workers, for more often than not they could observe and learn perfection in being shoulder to shoulder with the skilled. It was the long days' unaccustomed repetitive jobs for all of them which brought about downgradings from sheer monotonous boredom. The Tobey Furniture Co. in 1875 Chicago was one of several who received formal national commendation for its fine quality products. Joseph & William Allen of 1835 Philadelphia had become one of that Quaker City's most respected furniture emporiums by 1870. When the question arises of former "wellbred good taste" being lost during Victoriana, there is obviously no fault in the really beautiful pieces that were made, but rather their being hastily cluttered together without elbow room between and/or little informed regard given to related styles arrangements.

About 1850 Drummers (salesmen) began traveling to more populous areas, increasing their operations to the country's expansion, toting sample cases with miniatures of their wares, and shipping the larger pieces. Later in the century descriptive photographs and literature were available. Those miniatures and bigger objects can easily be mistaken by collectors as standard playroom pieces, but they warrant closer examination which should reveal their finely-precise and valuable made-to-scale perfection as Salesmen's Samples.

Characteristics

With furniture manufacturers from most of our then—34 states participating, the outstanding array of diversified exhibits at Philadelphia's 1876 Centennial only confirmed the period's inability to settle down to a definite look and declare, "This is Victorian...this is mine!" But it did stimulate interest in novelty items made from a variety of imported reeds and those for which patents had been issued, not for new designs, necessarily, but fore features that let them be rocked, rolled around, opened out, folded up, tilted, and so on. In this field George Hunzinger, renowned in 1850–1890 New York City, showed a walnut folding chair he'd patented in 1869. His machine inspired decorative ideas were mostly from pistons, cogs, knobs, and wheels in walnut with gilt and upholsterings. During an active 1860–1900 development of adjustable goods, highchairs were let down for rocking, handy settees with hinged ends folded out for longer couches, and chairs became recliners, following the ancient custom where the sparse furniture they did have contributed more than a single function. Manufacturers' or patent owners' names and dates appeared on most items. Among these makers, The American Chair Co. was active in Troy, New York along with the Sargent Manufacturing Co. in 1885 New York City, turning out adjustable reading chairs and recliners.

To some extent our whole country enjoyed the prevailing furniture trends. With the unrestrained opulences of Louis XV's French Court and the muted magnificences of Louis XVI's court, the natural emphasis on Louisiana was affected in varying degrees. Our lesser producing Southwest and Pacific Coasts were Spanish-inclined; the East Coast with New England, the Southland, and Midwest suggested the English. Most of the south still prefers rich dark wood tones and cool white appendages while easterners continue to enjoy warmer looking pink and chocolate variegated marble tops. Midwestern manufacturers, though fairly effusive themselves, did not try to attain the lush embellishments of the others. Spacious homes everywhere with high ceilings and airy rooms accommodated tall massive pieces. In the snowbelts where heating restricted such grand usage of space, smaller but no less ornate furniture was installed. The West had its Trophy styles into the early 1900's, chairs and setee benches, along with hatracks and other miscellaneous pieces, made from whole horns of elk, buffalo, and steers, the hides strong upholsterings. Fashioned earlier, these first came to wide attention around 1880 when the enthusiastic pleasure of President Lincoln for presentation pieces was historically publicized; President Theodore Roosevelt was photographed seated in a an animal horns chair; and a set was purchased for Scotland's Balmoral Castle.

Woods do not set an absolute style nor year. Imported mahogany and rosewood, long the favorites, were joined about 1855 by our American black walnut, which ruled in unison, so much that we often refer to those years as "The Age of Walnut." By the late 1880's walnut had been dangerously overcut. In the southeastern states holly dyed black could be an ebony substitute. Others used were maple, birch, ash, combined hard and soft woods, some stained to resemble the favorites. A bit of cherry and satinwood appeared. Curly, tiger, and birdseed maple, burl and crotch mahogany, and walnut were handsome veneers. With black walnut becoming less abundant, usage was extended to all walnut species. Native hardwoods in frontier pieces were stained brown or red; poplar was invariably painted. (To protect wood surfaces painting of furniture began several thousand years ago.) Pine, lightly used after 1850, wasn't knotty, clear sections still in vast supply. Southern makers liked cypress and hickory with occasional dogwood as those in other areas enjoyed using apple and pearwood.

Circular saw marks are an indication of post-1850 manufacturing; independent joiners and cabinetmakers used straight saw blades. For greatest strength mortise and tenon joints continued to be used for joining massive headboard units, these dominating Victorian bedrooms, replacing highpost canopies. Beds had straight lines until mid-century, when many footboards displayed halfround curved corners.

Bolts held together cast iron furniture parts; nail and glues to a larger extent made 18th century dowels and woodpins obsolete. Machine made screws had even and regular spirals with blunt ends ca. 1815. Pointed screws were machine made after 1845, and countersunk screws first appeared on Spool Turned items. Dovetails are the corner joints of drawers, averaging about 1" in width in the earlier 1800's, uniform in size, four or five to a drawer. Factory dovetails have rounded ends, on a wide drawer looking somewhat like the buttoned over-scallops on a child's Sunday-best high buttoned shoes.

Folding chairs with cloth seats were a late 19th century idea while factory produced rocking chair arms had typically curved arms. Chairs were shaped or turned; shaped frames had concealed dowel joints with seat rails reinforced by nails or screws, carvings and crests cut out as part of the chairwood rather than applied. Turned chairs were not often pegged, socket joints were glued, seats solid or caned. In man's constant search for comfort, chairs, once a royal prerogative, were the first furniture parts produced by the new assembly line methods, in innumerable quantities, qualities, and styles...dictated by continuing large market volume.

Charles Tish in 1884 New York City made rosewood cabinets with exotic woods inlays, oriental looking. When other woods were becoming scarce, oak, which had declined with the Middle Ages, was again much in demand, stained darker. (Deep English Oak is sometimes confused with our native black walnut.) That in turn was shunted aside ca. 1890–1900 by a yellowish lacquer, achieving Golden Oak. But a quartered oak was by far the prettiest, and most costly, there being considerable cutting loss getting this ripply flecked grain. Beech, sycamore, and butternut–a species of walnut–were latecomers. From a deep stained acacia came small cabinets and chairs. But outside the towns, whatever best came to hand was utilized.

Upholstering was done in the most luscious velvets, gorgeous tints of reds and blues with some greens and golds, elegant satins, patterned and plain damasks, brocades, and brocatels, sometimes shot with gold or silver threads or both, and rocking chairs edged with fringes dripping to thick bright loomed carpets and Oriental rugs. Smallest size fruits, berries, and flowers denote earliest patterns. Just when wood framed tapestry fireguards or floorscreens had been nicely pigeon-holed as "medieval scenes are chiefly English," up pops one of Teutonic inspiration. Jeweled tubular "bugle" and round bands on woven fabrics, also fancied on widespread home needlework, flashed iridescently under prism-ladled garish or softer lamps. Tapestried firescreens were a must in all poorer households, but aside from embossed cast iron ones set in front of night-banked ashes, were more delightful than to behold than utilitarian. By 1870 plush coverings were in vogue, and in complete contrast to all such satisfying fabrics, a slick, prickly, shiny-black substance came to be. Combining linen and hairs from horses' tails and manes, this horsehair is said to be the most representative of all Victorian upholsterings. Terribly popular, its cold surfaces had two attributes...it promoted social conformity because occupants sat in the correct straightback position with both feet firmly planted on the floor (to keep from sliding off), AND the material wore, and it wore!

From 1840 to 1860 drawer pulls matched the furnitures' woods, plain round knobs, mushrooms, or 4" plus widths of well carved leaf, fruit, and flower clusters. From 1810 into the 1870's there was pressed glass, opalescent, clear, and white with rare cutglass on a few of the finest pieces. China knobs became desirable, especially on country items. After 1870 metal pulls consisted of large indeterminate patterns, fanciful plates, rectangular or smaller round ring bails attached. Ebonized "teardrops" had silver or brass collars; all are now copied, cutglass rarely.

Compressed paper pulp combined with size (glue) and resin called

PAPIER MACHE was briefly used as an inexpensive substitute for wood. Heavily lacquers, inlaid with mother of pearl, painted, or gilded, it was intricately formed into curious light chairs and firm or tilt top teatable tops. Noted as background material for 18th century portrait plaques of royalty, in Victorians it was soon appropriately made into small household mugs, funnels, and so on.

Easily broken slate converted into table and pedestal surfaces was introduced by a few makers, inexpertly painted to resemble marble. It was not well received.

In 1850 the Boston Iron Works, Samuel S. Bemnt & Co. of New York City, and Philadelphia's Robt. Wood & Co. manufactured superb cast iron furniture, the last working in Louis XV substyle. Popularly painted white for summertime-coolness, many had grape clusters; others were realistically finished leaves and branches. Carved wood patterns firmly pressed into damp sand were then lifted out, molten iron being poured into the imprinted designs. The absolute rage of the 1860's–1870's and able to withstand adverse climates, they were desirable outdoors and attractive indoors. It was profusely supplied in tables, hallstands, stools, garden seats, along with hatracks, and some parlor pieces. (Before the 1871 disastrous Chicago fire, iron was used for building facades, treated to resemble masonry, but iron crumbled under excessive heat. After the fire, rebuilding was done in masonry painted to resemble iron as accurately as possible.) Although 1840–1870 cast iron furniture was sold in maker-limited areas due to shipping weights, this presented no buyers' problems since so many foundries were widely operating.

Bamboo from stems of a giant tropical weed was imported for flimsy furniture until in 1870 it was discovered that simulated materials were just as effective and much more durable. Birdseye maple was ideal, lathe turned, then left natural, bronzed, and stained.

Bentwood was in favor after Michael Thonet, who had perfected the process of steambending solid wood in 1856 Vienna, opened an 1874 New York City factory. With native beechwood he made chairs, all sorts of stands, and baby carriages.

Victorians loved all reed items from rattans, willow strips, and cane, to the pliable wicker. Ships arriving in the China trade had long used rattan as dummage, throwing it away after cargos were unloaded. An 1844 Boston grocer, Cyrus Wakefield, noticed this. After lengthy experimentation he was eventually able to process the rattan for furniture construction. Begun actively after 1865, it peaked in 1890 as with large output of baby carriages, music holders, chairs, rockers, and stools.

Spiderweb wicker, tightly woven into elaborate patterns on light weight wood frames is still more beautiful and collectible (and scarcer and more expensive) than looser weaves and general heaviness see after 1900. The many 1875 Basket Chairs had loose cushions or button upholsterings. Mentzer Read & Co., Grand Rapids manufacturers, actively competed in this field with Jones Smith of New York City.

Classification

The restless Victorians kept adopting whatever styles they believed more fitting to their steadily improving economic positions, ever seeking increased visual expression. No single Revival influence was permanent; to many ran concurrently for strict cataloging. Those firmly implanted in the first years of the 1800's with every expectation of continuing indefinitely found themselves becoming shaky as modes from still other times paralleled and then supplanted them in the way all fashions change. Overlapping periods flowed smoothly, the new never abruptly usurping the old. The TRANSITIONAL PERIOD of Early Victoriana 1830–1850 means the passage from one stage of development to another. Specifically, the 18th century New York City shop of one of our finest cabinetmakers, Scotsman Duncan Phyfe (wider advertised and thus better known than others just as skilled in Pittsburgh, Annapolis, Baltimore, and other cities during 1790–1847) best illustrates such transition from our 1800–1815 FEDERAL PERIOD into our 1800–1845 EMPIRE PERIOD. Phyfe's light touch with Directoire in 1830 bowed to Empire, ponderous except for dainty sidechairs.

Early in the 1840's ROCOCO or Victorian "modern" gradually phased out the graceful LATE CLASSICAL (PILLARS & SCROLLS), one of the first styles machine mass produced. Usually, a rich mahogany veneer grain-matched over pine and other such inexpensive woods, Rococo continued on, simply and easily made, popular in the 1950's in modified and combined forms, but still largely featuring their continuous stiles and rails construction.

Preferring such heavier forms of ancient days EMPIRE (displaced in turn by LOUIS XV REVIVAL–ROCOCO) had fewer curves, giving us instead deeply carved eagles, lyres, acanthus leaves, pineapples, crowns, and animals' feet and legs in cherry and mahogany with painted poplar, pine, oak, ash and shadings accurately resembling metals, mostly bronze. Because of its popular appeal in Victoriana and its strong distinctive touches throughout most of the century, EMPIRE deserves respectful attention.

Along with the REVIVALS, new movements began to appear in a "different" look after 1876. A COLONIAL REVIVAL, for instance, was factory copies of original colonial furniture but incorporating Victorian decorations. Skilled cabinetmakers also entered the field with many superior results.

The functional lines of MISSION FURNITURE developed by Gustav Stickley and copied by his brothers in 1895 Grand Rapids stressed straight lined dark stained oak with leather and accenting bright fabric upholsterings. The idea of our once well recognized MORRIS CHAIR, created by the English W. Morris, and extensively made in his own factory as a specialty item from 1875 to about 1940, was seized by Victorian makers here. They turned out countless AMERICAN MORRIS CHAIRS, especially in Grand Rapids. And there were the many changing faces of the ARTS & CRAFTS

MOVEMENT, as well as ART NOUVEAU, this last customarily included, although in its peak from 1895 to 1905, furniture concerns were secondary to its concentration on decorative and functional art and architecture. However, each of these did evolve with extreme changes so late in the century and did continue too far into the 1900's beyond the period's American guidelines to be herein illustrated as typically lavish Victorians.

Two words have surfaced with collectors: SUBSTYLE and ECLECTIC. Substyle translates as underdone, below the original. Eclectic means choosing what seems to be the best from various types. These last are the toughies to identify, some entirely undefinable, neither is easy. While "American Victorian" plainly and accurately covers all of those 19th century furniture years, present dedication to involved explanations demands more. Three phases, then, may be chosen: Early, Mid, and Late. With that understood, for even greater simplification, they are herein designated as EARLIER VICTORIAN and LATER VICTORIAN. After the formal revivals, those styles first named for their most evident traits or for their principal makers are described. Circa dates given by owners are as generally accepted; again, these vary to individual research and/or opinion.

Earlier Victorian
1820–1850
Gothic Revival
1815–1880–Crested in the 1840's

Originating in 12th century France, Gothic spread over Europe in cathedral architecture. Formal American Gothic is now sparse on tables. Bookcases, sideboards, hall, church, and fraternal chairs may be found. It is definitely ecclesiastical with raised applied moldings, steeple turned finials, pointed arches, overhanging cornices, standard seats of wood, fabric or cane with high frame backs, and ancient heraldic designs, usually in oak, with occasional black walnut, rosewood, and some mahogany crotch veneer. Among the early cabinetmakers, George J. Henkels whose 1850–1870 warehouse was opposite Independence Hall, included maple and satinwood. When Phineas T. Barnum of circus fame sponsored the Swedish Nightingale's 1850–1852 visit to Philadelphia, Henkels and his partner, Daniel Pabst, presented Jinny Lind with a low Gothic substyle bed having ornate draperies and side canopies. To the partners, of course, thereafter it was their Jinny Lind Bed. More commonly known by that name is a type of spool variations turnings. John Jeliff, being a talented artist, first made stencil sketches of his furniture designs, featuring broad button upholstered seats and trumpet legs, carried out in rosewood and walnut. He also worked in Rococo and Louis XVI until 1890, in Newark, New Jersey. Alexander and Frederick Roux were famous in 1850 New York City for their leaf carvings. Manufacturers Joseph Meeks & Sons established there in 1820 supplied a set of twelve chairs to the White House in 1846–1847, which President Lincoln later placed in his Cabinet Room. Meeks dispensed catalogue posters and sold widely, even to South American dealers.

Rococo (Louis XV) Revival
1840–1870

Considered modern in the 1840's this gaudily luxurious baroque was daringly accepted. After 1850 it was happily reflected in anything and everything far past furniture...cloth, iron, porcelain, and glass items... elegant or humbly basic. Our Rococo Revival represented all that was grandly American Victorian with its carved grapes and roses, finger moldings, broken and exaggerated pediments, curved legs ending in ornamental or grotesque feet, and graceful serpentine frames in rosewood and black walnut with some mahogany and cherry. Upholstering became popular with the advent of matched sets...parlor, bedroom/chamber, dining 'en suite,' and rocking chairs. For the parlor a Setee, a Gentleman's Chair, and a slightly smaller Lady's in matching or related fabrics were often joined by a plush rocking chair with mammoth fringes. Through the years as coverings wore, new patterns could have put have been put over the old, and finding such, to carefully peel off the layers down to the original would be an adventure in learning the tastes of the owners and materials available to them. J.S.L. Babbs in his steampowered factory on Boston's Albany Street in the 1850's, Gould & Co. in 1857 Philadelphia, and S.J. John of Cincinnati, all specialized in parlor and bedroom sets, the last advertising to attract the affluent Ohio–Mississippi river's trades, and stressing "Fashionable Furniture and Loo Tables'(Loo a popular card game of the era). The most fabulous sets were of three favorite woods, while manufacturers of less expensive pieces used oak, dyed maple, and chestnut. Prudent Mallard, coming from Sevres, France, was considered the most experienced of all New Orleans cabinetmakers, eventually opening a furniture factory operation until 1860, seeking the patronage of wealthy plantation owners and substantial townsfolk. Another very respected craftsman there was French immigrant Francois Seignouret, specializing in Louis XV chairs and handsome armoires, working for about 30 years from 1820. The story goes that his letter S was carved somewhere among the embellishments of each piece he made. But by far the most distinguished cabinetmaker in Rococo Revival was New York City's German emigre' John Henry Belter, operating his own cabinet factory from 1844 to 1864. Belter patented his process of wood lamination in 1856, steamheating under pressure from 3 to 4 up to 16 paper thin sheets of preferred rosewood, making his base for stronger intricate carvings and overall greater durability. (Egyptians had known the secret of wood lamination, using ages before on their sarcophagi.) Belter liked high arched pediments in massive architectural expressions, applied moldings and ornamentation, and burled walnut veneer panels, his furniture never inexpensive — then or now. Most cased pieces, along with his tables, have marble tops. Belter kept two chairs in one of his second story display windows, every couple of weeks throwing one to the street below as proof of their endurance. Chairs were made in limited quantity, plain backs without a seam down the entire center, said to have been one way his imitators escaped patent infringements. Belter created from black walnut, rosewood, some oak, cherry, and also burnished gold leaf finishes. Drawers were often maple-lined. To date there are no known Belter reproductions. Very proud and secretive, Belter in his later years angrily destroyed his patented (ply-wood) chair molds because of subtle encroachments and his frustrations at trying to preserve fine individual work and integrity against overwhelming mass production competition. His is a classic example of the talented successful woodmaster bowing to mechanical progress, for after Belter's death just prior to 1865, his brothers-in-law, who had been working with him in lamination carvings, tried to keep the business going but were forced into bankruptcy at the close of 1867. Chas. Baudouine operated his large factory there 1845–1860, making similar pieces, using cabriole legs, whorled feet, serpentine curves, and handcarved solid embellishments glued into place. A Seibrecht produced parlor sets from 1850 into the late 1880's in Louis XV substyle, but his solid carvings and crests were not pierced cut. After 1865 Rococo was heavily manufactured. Grand Rapids Marts sold parlor sets in simplified versions during those same years. Black horse hair coverings were much admired with Hampton & Sons specializing there after 1850.

Spool Turned

1815...well under way by 1830...largely made 1850–1865...in smaller quantities to 1880.

The true spool turnings were made by trained factory workmen using multiple blade power driven lathes, converting straight wood into continuous repeating units, these bored for spindles, or sliced apart into halves to order. Today what we sometimes deem spools can be the attractive button, mushroom, or ball turnings, also from factory specialists. With split halves glued or nailed on so many cased pieces, these turnings grew in usage until by 1840 some factories more profitably retired from general furniture making and only supplied such turnings to other makers. On the best quality items buttons and similar turnings were cut as part of a turned post rather than added as an applied trim. Birch, maple, and native hardwoods were painted or stained to copy the cabinetmakers' black walnut and rosewood. While miscellaneous pieces may be found, most were whatnots, washstands, tables, chairs, and fanciful shelves with beds far in the foreground. Bobbin turnings decorated lower priced items, chiefly those for bedrooms. Overall lighter in size and appearance to the more elegant Victorian, spool head and foot boards were customarily the same height; wooden slats appeared holding mattresses; and used for the first time were countersunk screws. Aside from the Jenny Lind Beds of Spool Turnings, many other turned pieces have been so named. During the 1850's particularly in Boston, beds advertised as "iron butter turned" were widely sold, but only the posts were cast with round imitative turnings. Spool Turned is the most appropriately a country style...to be cherished!

The elusive ELIZABETHAN REVIVAL during 1840–1850, due to its ball turnings, might be loosely grouped with the Spool Turned Period, although the individual turnings were much larger and more spiral twistings were incorporated. With small likeness to the original Elizabethan furniture, it was still widely admired in Victoriana. Definitely luxurious pieces, they were prominent in ebonizing, rich tapestry upholsterings, and generous fringes. Among cabinetmakers, Henry Jenkins & Son restricted their output, working in rosewood and mahogany, now and then reaching into Louis XV. Their attention was on highback clergy type chairs and large handsome spirals. At Cincinnati in 1859 Wm. Cremsey made and widely advertised rocking and parlor chairs.

Cottage Style
1845–1900

Considered a novelty–that gained instant acceptance–the birch, pine, and maple used covers a vast number of bedroom sets, sidechairs, and such, which, along with Spool Turnings, motivated expanding factories for inexpensive mass production. The homier woods were easily painted, stenciled, falsewood grained, and gilt decorated. In fact, most of the woods required such finishes. Chair seats were often caned, but caned backs on Cottage chairs are unusual. Merrian & Parsons as Cottage Furniture Manufacturers & Dealers shipped chair parts from their Boston warehouse on Fulton Street. Cottage Furniture is not to be considered cheap or inferior. In 1876 Horace J. Farmington, New York City, sold rich ornamented gold and white enameled Room Sets, although his purpose was still the reason for the evolution of Cottage Styles..."pretty forms at moderate prices."

Later Victorian
1850–1900
Renaissance Revival
1855–1880

Extremely popular, with an almost smothering Germanic flavor, this period saw the important rise of marble surfaces. In preferred black walnut with many burl veneer panels, there were medallions impressively treated with contrasting inlays and gilt incisings. Fruitwood grips, machine made carved pendant pulls, wide trims and scrolls were used along with brilliant upholsterings. Unusual too were imitation or split dining and parlor table pedestals (so they could be pulled out for additional "leaves" to be added for extra length), rectangularly squared chair backs and seats, and heavier front legs. Cabinetmaker Thos. Brooks was active in 1872 Brooklyn, New

York. Already catering to his wealthy clientele in the fashionable manner of Louis XV Revival, New Orleans' Prudent Mallard included Renaissance Revival, while Grand Rapids, Michigan manufacturers produced a great many pieces, now often called "Grand Rapids Renaissance."

Louis XVI Revival
1865–1880

Easier to identify, this second French influence differs from the first Louis XV in its large round turnings at the top of front slender legs. Ebonizing was popular, as well as mahogany, some oak, walnut, and rosewood. Inset marble tops graced parlor tables and stands, while carved masks, upholstered ovals and keystone arches ornamented other wood crest frames. Among New York City's masters, Leon Marcotte during the 1860's produced excellent ebonized maple and fruitwood pieces with rare gilt and and bronze metal trims; Herter Bros. were importantly established by 1875, often using cherrywood with marble tops, known for Eastlake and Japanese trends as well 1870–1880; and Pottier & Stymus in 1870 were commended for such fine decorations on their exhibits in the 1876 Centennial. Grand Rapids factories worked largely on this substyle.

Jacobean Revival
1870's

With factory-mades so rapidly increasing, makers searched for new inspirations. This substyle was thought to have considerably contributed to a loss of the widespread French elegance, furniture taking on, instead, a solidly rigid look in oak and walnut. Simplicity in dots and brief panels (dashes) were repeated, beveled edges replaced beautiful scrolls, flowers and leaf sprays cut in outline, while flat, wide, decorative moldings were twisted into designs reminiscent of 17th century Jacobean strapwork. Turned spindles, other than spool types were used wherever possible (incredibly) on furniture of most categories. Wood skirts were on tables and shelves; manufacturers everywhere were kept busy filling orders.

During those 1870's fussy whatnots arrived, imperative in homes, perfect for showing off the countless beautiful and/or ugly bricabac treasured by Victorian homemakers.

American Eastlake Styles
1870–1900

In those years a sincere English architect-writer, Charles Locke Eastlake, himself partial to Gothic Revival, published (prissy) principles for polite behavior and his own thoughts on good taste in furniture and furnishings. All these aided at giving proper guidance to Americans, whom he considered to be sadly lacking in such niceties.

Always alert for real or imagined self-improvement, the earnest American Victorians in turn avidly embraced his coy suggestions for etiquette. And our manufacturers, ever prompt to exploit any popular influence to their sales advantages, achieved a new look in their wares which today is easily recognizable once it becomes familiar. Mr. Eastlake was not entirely pleased that his name was given to our colonies efforts, but it was, and there it remains. His real feeling was that simplicity and usefulness were the basic elements needed in furniture, in itself an honest approach. However, our explosions of interpretations did bring forth reduced massiveness, rectilinear lines, very effective accenting of dark woods with inlays on panels of naturally light colored woods, sometimes vice versa; and although still happily squandering decorations, it was slightly less than before. Oak, walnut, ash, poplar, maple, cherry, and chestnut were most common, with ivory, contrasting color woods and shell inlays. Crests were scalloped or pointed, machine carvings leaf and geometric patterns, edges reeded, various sawtooths, shallow plain and gilded incisings, and handles mostly bails on stamped metal plates or pendant brass rings and teardrop pulls. Multiple turned spindles were added to simple items. Furniture line and their manufacturers increased even more dramatically.

Thus, still reflecting the moods of the people, who were tapering down from unnatural posturings into more relaxed behavior, their furnishings in turn subsided. Beautiful furniture long relegated to dampish cellars and cobwebby garrets and sheds has been carried out into the sunlight of acceptance, to reign again in this second of its centuries.

And a wonderfully extraordinary period of our history closed at the dawn of the 1900's, leaving to still anther era its own evolving furniture fashions.

Beds, Cradles, Cribs, Carriages

HEADBOARD, worn Renaissance substyle in walnut and burl veneer; massive crest-broken pediment; ornate uprights; ca.: mid-century; H. 9'. $2,400.00

Bonnet top walnut Rococo substyle HEADBOARD; applied floral carving. $2,300.00

Eastlake influenced walnut and burl HEADBOARD about 8½' tall; reeded sections, incisings, and carvings. $900.00 – 1,300.00

LOW POSTS of mahogany TWIN BEDS, Colonial Revival. Pineapples are one of the earliest emblematic fruits of hospitality, much favored on furniture, staircase newell posts, and artifacts of materials other than wood. $1,800.00 per pair.

Rococo Revival BED attributed to Belter; walnut with crotch veneer; pierced carvings and crested Indian with feathers; ebonizing; molded curved footposts; fullsized beds average L. 70"–74"; W. 53"–66"; this one H. 8'; Ft. H. 30". $5,500.00+

Mrs. Ulysses S. Grant's guest BED when visiting Magnolia Manor, Cairo, Illinois; Rococo elements in rosewood with crotch veneers; pierced urn tops; finger moldings frame ovals; rounded footboards; H. 10'; Ft. H. 3'. No Price Available.

Pierced cut; acanthus crest; projection top squared posts; walnut and burl BED; Rococo Revival; curved footposts; H. 8"; Ft. H. 30". $4,400.00 – 4,500.00

Rococo substyle pierced and shell carvings decorating mahogany and burl BED; hexagon posts with heavy feet and lighter headboard finials; H. 8"; Ft. H. 36". No Price Available.

26

TWIN BED; Rococo Revival in walnut and burl;
pierced and applied carvings; tulip crest; ca. 1860.
"Summer" beds grew in popularity about 1840,
two under one canopy, then independently emerg-
ing: H. 6 ½'. $3,500.00 – 4,000.00 per pair.

TWIN BED, walnut with applied moldings and burl crest; square head-board posts, curved at foot; H. 7'; Ft. H. 30". $1,800.00 – 1,900.00 per pair.

BED with applied roundel and veneer panels on walnut, squared grooved posts; H. 6'6"; Ft. H. 24".$750.00 – 800.00

Urns achieve a graceful balance on walnut BED with deeper burl applied panels; shell crest interrupts finger molding of center cutout, winged sides; bonnet pediment; H. 10'; Ft. H. 36". $1,850.00 – 2,200.00

Sleigh variation of a country BED with Empire lines; rosewood and crotch veneer with gilt; Equal 38" H. head and footboards; low to fit under rural ceilings. Courtesy Magnolia Manor. No Price Available.

Cottage/Country style "Cannonball" low posts walnut BED, ca.: 1860 – 65; low footrail knobs held rope lacings taut with bedwrenches – replaced with slats. Beds among country pieces were least affected by changing Victoriana. $1,800.00 – 2,000.00

Low Country style stained poplar BED; sausage and flat ball turnings;ca. 1860 – 70. $650.00 – 750.00

Spool and ball turnings full size BEDSTEAD in walnut; has slats; countersunk screw construction; molded headboard crest; Jinny Lind type with equal height four posts approx. 7' while headboard is about 40" high. $2,100.00 – 2,400.00

31

Deepstained local wood lowposts equal H. 48" BED, Spool turned; third quarter of the 1880's. $700.00 – 750.00

Fancy YOUTH BED, ca.: 1850 – 75: walnut with spindles and turnings; H. 44" Ft. H. 20". Courtesy Magnolia Manor. No Price Available.

Eastlake style three Pc. walnut with burl veneer; marble tops and splashboard; teardrop pull screws extend through drawers factory dovetailed; BED H. 8'; DROPFRONT DRESSER H. 6'; WASH-STAND H. 38". $4,200.00 – 4,500.00 per set.

BEDROOM SET; walnut; burl veneers; machine modified Renaissance and S-bowed drawers; applied trims, incisings, marble, brass fixtures, and tilting bevel glasses. Such mirror-back Commodes were liked in many areas, Pennsylvania for one. The mirrors removed and hung separately in various other regions. The Set a 1980 Dealer-sold @ $3,000.00, valued to $4,500.00 – 4,800.00; Bed. H. 8'; other pcs. H. 7' approx.

34

Solid Brass BABY'S BED: ca.: 1890 – 95; sides lower; H. 38", L. 54"; brass and iron beds grew in popularity after 1880. $1,750.00 – 2,000.00 (Varies by region)

Spool turned stained ash CHILD'S DAYBED; ca.: 1850; mushroom turnings and spade feet; ends fold for storage and uprights brace pillows. $350.00 – 400.00

WINDOW SEAT/DAYBED, walnut and original caning; ca.: 1870 – 80; adjustable ends can hold pillows or overall thick cushion; ends with carrying handles; a Country Doctor carried it in his horsedrawn buggy making house calls; open L. 54"; W. 20". $375.00 – 400.00

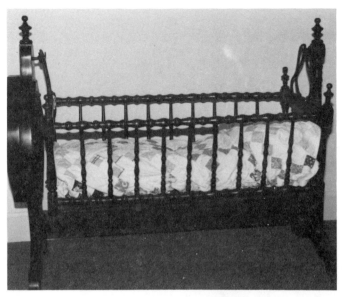

Rare SELF ROCKING CRA-
DLE; walnut with true spool
and other turnings; swings on
iron hangers; casters. original
paper label: A.D. Crane Co.,
Patented 1852; clock type
brass winding key seen in
foreground on "drum" enclos-
ing mechanical parts. $975.00
– 1,200.00

CHILD'S CRIB; walnut with burl; uncommon caned head and footboard centers: ca. last quarter of the 1800's. $675.00 – 750.00

DOLL'S BED, walnut with darker glued on panels; bonnet top. $350.00 – 550.00

Massive DOLL'S BED, Louis XV Revival with shells, cherubs, and moldings applied. $600.00 – 750.00

Baby Carriages

Sears & Roebuck in their 1897 catalogue offered them for a modest $2.45 to a very elegant model @ $40. Rubber tires standard on the more expensive and $2 a set on cheaper. Handles were bentwood; axles and springs finest Bessemer steel; linings silk or plush with puffing for added comfort; the strongest reeds; and patented brakes foot controlled.

Deepstained maple CARRIAGE with bentwood and reeds; wood wheels; restored silk. $550.00 – 575.00

Elaborate PHOTOGRAPHER'S CARRIAGE with silk fashioned into patterns even on outer sides; fringe; ruffled parasol sunshade on adjustable iron bar. $550.00 – 595.00

Woven wicker and reeds TWIN'S CARRIAGE, adjustable back
and foot basket; rubber tires and footbrake. $500.00 – 525.00

Single CARRIAGE; fancy woven reed and wicker with darker
design strip; footbrake. $350.00 – 400.00

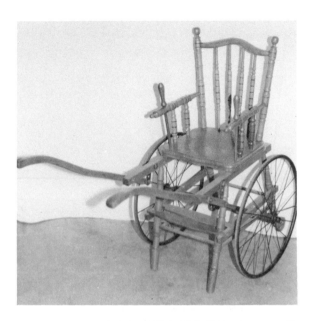

Maple RICKSHAW (STROLLER) for small
child; comb back; complicated. $275.00 – 350.00

DOLL'S CARRIAGE; ca.: 1870 – 80; stained maple and bentwood; wood wheels. $250.00 – 400.00

Stained maple DOLL'S CARRIAGE; as found; once had a fringed canopy and velvet upholstering; sleigh shaped body. $325.00 – 425.00

Bookcases, Bookstands, Desks, Desk Chairs, Secretaries

Walnut two pc. BOOKCASE, adjustable shelves have unusual edge applied moldings; original paper label: Paine's Furniture Co., Boston 1870; brass fixtures, generous cornice. Bookcases are now becoming attractive china cabinets. H. 6' 10"; W. 43". $1,200.00 – 1,500.00 (Average to area)

Walnut and burl BOOKCASE; two pcs. with useable open shelf above teardrop pulls drawers; metal crest set on bonnet top; H. 84"; W. 42". $1,200.00 – 1,500.00 (Average to area)

Applied carved LIONS' HEADS with cornice guard on Empire substyle walnut and burl BOOKCASE; brass knobs and well defined lions' feet on all four corners; H. 6' 2"; W. 38". Naturalistic patterns of animal carvings have reappeared from time to time since the furniture of the pre-Christians. $1,000.00 – 1,200.00

BOOKCASE with bureau drawers, fruitwood pulls;
walnut with applied burl; suitable for a child's
room; H. 54"; W. 36". $850.00 – 900.00

American Empire BOOKCASE-DESK; cherry with maple burl veneers; turned four feet all carry out carved pineapples also used at top and base of rope posts; pullout panels hold each side of writing shelf that lifts and unfolds forward; selfwood knobs and brass key escutcheons; H. 74"; W. 43"; D. 23". $3,000.00 – 3,500.00

Eastlake lines walnut and burl veneered dropfront BOOKCASE-DESK; deep incisings; embossed, reeded, beveled glass, brass fixtures; H. 6'; W. 30" $1000.00 – 1,200.00

Dear to the hearts of rural homemakers, being also available from mail order catalogues, ca.: 1890's, darker stained oak with quartered sections BOOK-CASE-DESK with candle rests, spindled gallery, applied edge moldings and beadings, dropfront desk and many storage spaces; one of the period's (Grand Rapids) prized models; H. 6½'; W. 42". $975.00 – 1,200.00

Eastlake style walnut and burl
BOOKCASE-DESK; dated 1873;
dropfront writing surface; boxtype
squared corners top; brass rings
bails; H. 78"; W. 38". $1,200.00 –
1,300.00

Rosewood BOOKCASE-SECRETARY,
Rococo Revival, ca.: 1850; deeply finger
molded bonnet top with pierced and solid
carvings; slant top lifts, pulls out and
down for flat writing surface; H. 9½'; W.
42". $2,500.00 – 2,750.00

Whorl foot, three wide splat, walnut BOOK-STAND for larger home library; iron adjustable rails held by wooden drum allow 30" open width; overall H. 40". Private Collection. No Price Available.

BOOK/MAGAZINE
RACK with carrying han-
dle in walnut; Eastlake
style, embossed flower
panel, fretwork, and iron
side rails for space
adjustment; ca.: 1880's.
$350.00 – 400.00

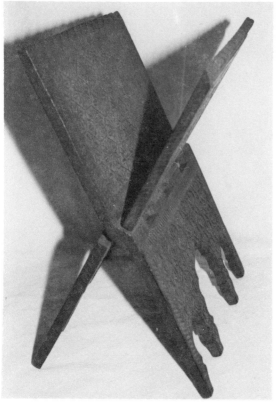

Stained popular DESK
BIBLE RACK, entirely
geometric design
embossed with grooved
sides; dovetail meshed
two pieces for desired
size adjusting; Moorish
influence. $150.00 –
175.00

Rare BUTLER'S DESK; walnut and burl veneer
inlays; sides and full interior birdseye maple;
ebony fruits, carved crest, and heavy finger moldings applied; dropfront panel (pseudo drawer
fronts) lowers to form leather top work surface and
reveals narrow inside drawer; turned stiles and
finials; borrows from the Renaissance; H. 8½'; W.
54"; D. 25". $4,200.00 – 4,600.00

William S. Wooten's KING OF DESKS...WELLS FARGO...superior grade, walnut with burl veneers, and a fine detailed gallery. Deep arched top doors open to disclose extensive storage sections. The patented green cardboard boxes only in the right door compartment is a Wooten characteristic. When the center dropdesk panel is lifted to form the flat closure, thus, exposed from the bottom side are delicate but firmly incised and gilded fan designs on lighter colored burl; drawer pulls are selfwood mushrooms, while functional fixtures are heavily etched brass. Casters made rolling easy and the desk can be overall locked in individual areas with the original keys. These desks are considered blue chip investments, that which had belonged to Queen Victoria offered in the 1978 Christmas Catalogue of Neiman-Marcus at Dallas, Texas for $150,000. This one was offered for sale in October 1979 at $16,000 and was sold. UP is the indicator.

Securing a patent Oct. 6, 1874, Wooten's Indianapolis, Indiana factory was in business until about 1884, in 1876 making around 150 desks a month. All had rotary piers, roll and flat tops, banking models, and with a few smaller ladies' size Wells Fargo types. John D. Rockefeller, Joseph Pulitzer, and President Grant were among the buyers. Prices averaged $90.00 to $750.00 with ordinary, standard, extra-grade, and superior models, prices of each geared to the embellishments. Costs have now risen with no prospect of declining...especially since there are only seven known examples of superior models, less than 24 extra grades, and three of the rare ladies'. $16,000.00 – 18,000.00

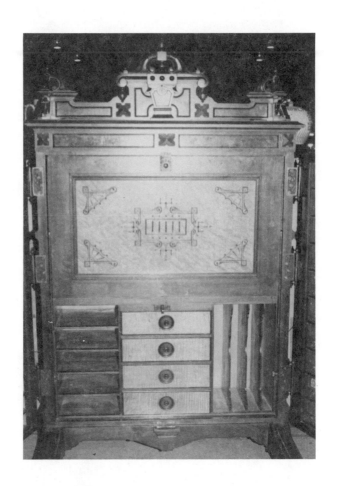

Walnut and burl American termed DAVENPORT DESK, invented by the English Mr. Devenport as a writing box over a side-drawers of side-doors cabinet. Here are three side drawers, large pendants, leather top, and shaped bracket supports; H. 36"; W. 30"; D. 26". $975.00 – 1,250.00

DAVENPORT DESK; walnut and burl; leather top; fretwork gallery; side doors; H. 34". W. 30"; lifttop. Courtesy Magnolia Manor. No Price Available.

Walnut DESK; burl drawer fronts with wood grips; turned and fluted split posts; top lifts up and out for flat writing surface; L. 54"; H. 33"; D. 20½". $2,200.00 – 2,800.00

CUSTOMADE LIFT FRONT DESK; walnut; inlaid and applied burl panels; curved top lifts out and down for flat writing space; rare birds-eye maple interior; at rear of lacy brass arched knee space are two doors concealing storage areas – this an unusual feature; ornate brass pulls; handcarved wood grip and knobs. $4,200.00 – 4,600.00

Cherry S-ROLL TOP DESK; deeply cut leaves and shells; applied wood grips carved as squared animals' masks; original brass key; extra small shelves pull out from each surface side. H. 52"; W. 46"; D. 28". $3,800.00+

Cherry S-ROLL TOP DESK; curved sides fold back on hinges so pieces can be pulled out to make extended small functional shelves; brass plate: Daten-Dunton Desk Co., Boston, Mass., U.S.A.; Pat. dated Aug. 14, 1894; H. 50"; W. 48"; D. 28". $3,000.00 – 3,300.00

FALLFRONT DESK; walnut, iron grips, gallery; turned and grooved all four legs; a Schoolmaster's in one area and a Plantation Desk in another; ca.: 1860 – 70. Eastlake style. $675.00 – 750.00

Leather writing surface walnut S-ROLL TOP DESK; concave bracket drawer stiles; incisings; metal pulls; H. 50"; W. 48"; D. 28". $2,600.00 – 2,750.00

Desk Chairs

DESK CHAIR, combined walnut and burl; rocks and revolves; carved wide splat on bowed for comfort back; note width graduated arm; incisings; restored caning. H. 42"; W. 25"; D. 24".$550.00 – 750.00

Bentwood oak (when the wood was green) SWIVEL ARMCHAIR for DESK ; cast iron post; center baluster firms back; ca.: 1870's; H. 40"; W. 25"; D. 23". $395.00 – 425.00

CYLINDER SECRETARY, combined black walnut and burl; barrel roll lifts for writing surface and filing sections; teardrop pulls; H. 8'; W. 48". $2,500.00 – 2,750.00

Eastlake type CYLINDER SECRETARY in walnut with rope brand below sawtooth – pierced cut – applied carvings cornice; uncommon left side door compartment rather than right side; H. 8½'; W. 42"; D. 24". $2,600.00 – 2,800.00

CYLINDER SECRETARY, walnut and burl veneers; deep incisings and reedings; top lifts, sliding back on rails under liftoff bookcase cabinet; H. 8½'; W. 40"; D. 24" widest part. $2,800.00 – 3,000.00

Side view to show contours of a CYLINDER SECRETARY, walnut and burl veneers; adjustable shelves indicate this is a new feature of the machine age; uncommonly locks at middle top of cylinder instead of at the base between the lift knobs. H. 8'7"; W. 40"; D. approx. 24" at roll. $2,800.00 – 3,000.00

Chairs – Side, Arm, Rocking, High

Competition among mushrooming factories was so keen no measures were so spared to rank foremost in the industry. One northern banker reportedly designed his chairs by hiring people to sit in snowbanks, transferring those impressions to his drawing boards; others sent their designers to study abroad in a dozen countries.

Side Chairs

Lowseat SLIPPER CHAIR attributed to Belter; pierced carved laminated rosewood; paired designs of fruit and scrolls with framing sides anchored to the seatback; front legs only have casters, typical of American Louis XV Revival pieces; original needlework; H. 43"; W. 18½"; D. 18". $1,850.00

SLIPPER CHAIR, Elizabethan Revival in walnut and burl;
turned front leg annulets and bulbs; shell crest with Indian feathers on its shield is joined internally to the wide-molded broken
pediment; original tapestry on coiled springs; stylized design
framed with molded oval resting on stayrail, seatback braced
with carved demi-arms; variations of this style were made for
decades. $1,400.00 – 1,500.00 +

SLIPPER CHAIR; original upholstering; Louis XVI sub-style in walnut; tulip crest divides curved top; Rococo type splayed rear legs continue the vertical sides; beading; knee carvings on front cabriole legs (Queen Anne influence); H. 38"; W. 18"; D. 16" (in reduced quality they were made in Cottage Styles dating from the 16th century. Conveniently low for ladies to change footwear, they appeared first in finest quality around the 1710 years of Queen Anne's reign.) $650.00 – 800.00

Renaissance Revival SLIPPER CHAIR; walnut with burl; long carved tassels; original cover; H. 37"; W. 22"; D. 15". $650.00 – 800.00

Low SIDE CHAIR; provincially also a BUSTLE or HOOPSKIRT chair whereon crinoles would spread out unhampered by standard arms; ca.: 1872; Renaissance Revival; walnut and red velvet; burl panels; finial and tasseled uprights. H. 36½"; W. 22". D. 18". $450.00 – 650.00

Black walnut Renaissance Revival SIDECHAIR; lady's head crest with mid-century side-curls; original tapestry; cup turned front legs; H. 38"; W. 23"; D. 20". $550.00 – 750.00

Pierced cut and solid carvings on rosewood framing delicate hand needlework of SIDECHAIR; original all the way. Matched sets, particularly in this fine quality of six or more, are scarce; Louis XV substyle. $2,800.00+

Velvet original upholstery tufted SIDECHAIR; Louis XV substyle; crested medallion frame on balloon curves fastened to seatback frame; ca.: mid-century. $550.00+

Always solid — not laminated BALLON BACK CHAIRS by 1860 had become ordinary seating pieces. Richly carved crest rail of a mahogany SIDECHAIR. Courtesy Magnolia Manor. No Price Available.

Serpentine legs indicate Transitional from Empire into mid-century 1800's with their Late Classical (Pillar & Scroll) cabriole lines, popular in 1830 with a Boston cabinetmaker, Samuel Gragg (noted for his bentwood chairs); thence into the 1850 – 60's, so much in favor they were among the first leg styles factory produced. Flower crestrail carved mahogany, slipseat BALLOON BACK CHAIR; reupholstered; Rococo substyle. $395.00+

Belter type rosewood Louis XV Revival SIDECHAIR; damask restored; pierced cut fruit and scrolls of crest and splat are framed with balloon curves whose whorl ends fit onto the seatback; deep serpentine apron and cabriole legs finger molded. Courtesy Magnolia Manor. No Price Available.

Simply but prettily carved fruit crested balloon back walnut SIDECHAIR with serpentine stayrail; removable velvet seat. $375.00+

Rosewood Rococo substyle SIDECHAIR with original tapestry; ca. : mid-century; elegance in fruit carvings, in leaf motifs on stayrail, apron and cabriole knees. $375.00+

Walnut SIDECHAIR, fruit carvings top balloon back and serpentine stayrail; velvet slipseat; Rococo Revival. $375.00+

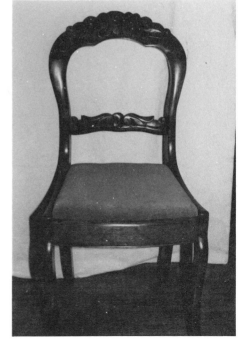

Slipseat walnut SIDECHAIRS; original hand needlework; balloon backs, grip cutout, carvings. $350.00+

Bold carvings on mahogany balloon back SIDECHAIRS; reupholstered. $350.00+

Carved balloon back Rococo substyle SIDECHAIRS in walnut; ready for players at a chess game set up on a burl bordered TABLE having a turned walnut post and ornate cast iron legs with whorl feet. Private Collection. No Price Available.

Original needlepoint mahogany SIDECHAIR; Rococo substyle balloon curves; carvings; finger grip; slipseat. $350.00

Walnut and burl BALLOON BACK SIDECHAIR; original needlepoint; simply carved braces (demi arms); Rococo substyle. $350.00

Walnut stained combined woods balloon back SIDECHAIR; Rococo substyle; reupholstered; simple decorations. $350.00

Two ballon SIDECHAIRS attributed to Detroit Chair Co., each one of a pair; ca.: 1870's; restored woven seat chair priced $125.00 – 150.00 each; the other with heavier overall construction – turnings and legs – with restored eyecaning priced $395.00+ for the pair; H. 34"; W. 18"; D. 19".

SIDECHAIR; elements of East-lake; deep stained walnut; needlepoint restored but adds to value; three-slat back with saw-tooth curved toprail down-curved; carrying handblock; short apron; chair is one of a set of six. $750.00 per set.

Factory Renaissance – Eastlake type legs walnut SIDECHAIR; ca.: 1860 – 80's widespread demi arms; H. 39". W. 21"; D. 22". $350.00

Maple SIDECHAIR with walnut burl panels in Eastlake manner; ready for eyecaning to the original; deeply incised splat: H. 35"; 20" Dia. of seat. $175.00 as is.

Curly maple SIDECHAIR; turned and grooved balusters and stretchers; continuous scroll cut crown. $225.00 (Varies by region)

In a set of 12 comfortable SIDECHAIRS for dining each slightly differs in size as a courtesy to the variations in people's measurements; some average about H. 32"; W. 22"; D. 24"; others approximate H. 30"; W. 20"; finger holds; ca.: 1880; walnut with eye caning. Courtesy Magnolia Manor. No Price Available.

Eastlake type SIDECHAIRS walnut stained combined woods, deeper burl trim; fretwork splats; set of four. $750.00 – 800.00

Mahogany Elizabethan Revival SIDECHAIR; flattened ball turnings; fretwork back frame peaks in a Gothic cross plush seat; H. 42"; W. 18½"; D. 17½". $225.00 – 300.00

Ebonized lightweight SIDECHAIR; restored velvet and gimp; dainty carvings applied to Gothic pointed arch; H. 41"; W. 17½"; D. 18". $200.00 – 275.00

Louis XV Revival SIDECHAIR; back uprights continue 1 pc. of wood each into rear legs; incised crest, burl panels, and original velvet; H. 38"; W. 18"; D. 19½"; walnut; ca.: 1870's. $350.00 – 375.00

Renaissance combined with Eastlake influence restored silk SIDECHAIR in walnut and burl; sawtooth and squared lines; reeding; fretwork; incisings; H. 40"; W. 19"; D. 21". Courtesy Magnolia Manor. No Price Available.

Eastlake walnut and burl
SIDECHAIR; ca.: 1870's; gilt
clover on center apron and
front turned legs at stretcher
mortise joinings; reeded
braces; H. 42"; W. 20"; D. 22".
$250.00 – 350.00

Eastlake SIDECHAIR; original horsehair covering (which
adds a hundred dollars if in
good condition); entire walnut
and burl frame deeply
embossed and incised; china
casters; tulip finials; H. 42";
W. 20"; D. 22". No Price
Available.

Late Empire Revival SIDECHAIR; all original; walnut, ca.: 1860; reeded and carved. $175.00 – 195.00

Rosewood SIDECHAIR; cutout-edge wide "Klismos Tablet" set at the top of side uprights; carved stayrail; knee projection Greek legs; slipseat restored velvet. The distinctly American innovation of ancient Greek Klismos – saber (scimitar shaped) legs and incurved backrests were derived from paintings seen on vases and urns as far back as the 5th century B.C. Empire substyle. $174.00 – 225.00 (in set of four)

Lyre fretwork splatback, broad tablet SIDECHAIR; curly maple; (these splatbacks are a feature resembling some of the Pennsylvania Dutch chairs). $200.00 – 225.00

Combined woods SIDECHAIR; walnut and curly maple; wide carved top has inside joining; urn shaped fretwork splat; restored slipseat. $250.00

Fancy SIDECHAIR in stained maple; ca.: 1860 – 80's; Empire influence in the Cottage manner; original stuffed buttoned velvet. Stuffing materials included cotton, horsehair, and/or straw. H. 33"; W. 20"; D. 18". $225.00

SIDECHAIR; Hitchcock type; all original; woven rushes seat; black painted with floral stencils in colors; turnings; button feet; side stretchers and rear legs plain turned; ca.: 1835 – 40. $800.00 – 950.00

Mahogany SIDECHAIR (Dining); leather seat; embossed splat; Bernard & Simonds Co. in Rochester, NY, numerous makers in Grand Rapids as elsewhere, produced these Colonial Revival eclectic styles. $650.00 – 700.00 (in set of six)

COMMODE (OR INVALIDS') CHAIR; stained local woods; velvet center liftop seat contains chamberpot; urn curved splat; seat is 16" from the floor. $195.00

Oak, partially quarter cut
SIDECHAIR; golden finish; flat
slats, grooves and turnings; quality factory work; H. 36"; W.
15½"; D. 16". $175.00

White painted poplar and wicker
SIDECHAIR; ornate detail; ca.: last
quarter 1800's; deepstained eye caning; H. 42". W. 17½" ; D. 17".
$175.00+

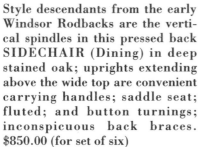

Style descendants from the early Windsor Rodbacks are the vertical spindles in this pressed back SIDECHAIR (Dining) in deep stained oak; uprights extending above the wide top are convenient carrying handles; saddle seat; fluted; and button turnings; inconspicuous back braces. $850.00 (for set of six)

Dark stained oak SIDECHAIR; braces; spindles; balusters; incisings; ca.: 1890's. $175.00

Arm Chairs

GENTLEMAN'S CHAIR; laminated rosewood; ca.: 1850; attributed to Belter; as all his chairs, the back is undivided with a seam; low seat and padded arms; Rococo substyle framing silk damask; ornately detailed pierced and solid carvings; finger grooved serpentines; H. 48½"; W. 25½" ; D. 28". $4,000.00 – 4,500.00

Belter type Rococo Revival GENTLEMAN'S ARMCHAIR in laminated rosewood; pierced cut and solid carvings included on apron and knees of short cabriole legs; deep finger groovings and serpentines; ca.: mid-century; H. 46"; W. 27½" ; D. 26". $3,400.00 – 3,800.00

Rococo substyle Belter type laminated rosewood LADY'S ARM-CHAIR; pierced cut and carved flowers and vines; low aproned seats and shortened cabriole legs to modestly accommodate hoop-skirts; ca.: mid-century; H. 42"; W. 26"; D. 27". $2,800.00 – 3,000.00

GENTLEMAN'S ARMCHAIR:
buttoned puffy arms and back;
Renaissance Revival with classical
influenced draped figures and
winged scrolls; H. 42"; W. 27"; D.
29"; original velvet; walnut. Private Collection. No Price Available

Louis XV Revival oval back
LADY'S ARMCHAIR; ca.:
1870; rosewood; serpentine
and vine tendril scrolls; H.
37"; W. 32"; D. 28". $445.00
– 650.00

Eastlake styling in 4th quarter of the century ARMCHAIR; walnut; sausage turnings, buttons, gilt, and incisings; H. 40"; W. 22"; D. 25". $375.00 – 400.00

Renaissance Revival ARM-CHAIR in walnut; glued on ebon trims; front legs cup turned; restored velvet; H. 38"; W. 21"; D. 23". $275.00 – 350.00

Fanciful stained maple and bentwood ARMCHAIR; ca.: last quarter of the century; caned seat about 16" from the floor; H. 34". $250.00 – 295.00

Deep stained maple WINDSOR type ARMCHAIR with solid pine saddle seat; heavier than 18th century version; bowed top a good headrest; overall comfortable; seat 16"–17" from floor; fretwork splat; many being reproduced. In 1885 – 90 Fitchburg, MA the Walter Heywood Chair Co.'s catalogue, aside from their other styles, showed about 20 different adaptations of the Windsors alone. $750.00 – 900.00

Maple ARMCHAIR; original eyecaning; ca.: 1865; carved roses crest; plain turned stretcher sides and rear; H. 38½"; W. 18½"; D. 20". $250.00 – 295.00

Arrowback plain and quarter cut oak deepstained ARMCHAIR; these factory made speed-assembled wood chair parts, chiefly around 1870 and later, resulted in many styles constructed of local woods in just about every smaller city in our country, many firms specializing in caned seat categories; these popular in Boarding houses, for instance. One of a pair. $225.00

ARMCHAIR; walnut; all original; Gothic Revival; plush upholstering with heraldic coat of arms; spires and fretwork; foyer type; special order category; Shaw, Applin & Co. of 1880 Boston, MA advertised such formal pieces. Private Collection. No Price Available

LODGE, FRATERNAL, WRITING ARMCHAIR; dark stained oak; saddle seat; embossing and lighter wood inlays at apron; 'Grand Rapids Jacobean;' H. 50"; W. 24"; D. 26". $275.00 – 300.00

Country makers did turn out a few novelty chairs but mid-western and eastern factories produced most in all materials in urban centers and shipped them all over the country. As an example, this is a gilded sloping back CHAIR seen in restoration; canvas covered coil springs have a restored loose cushion; huge split grooved buttons complete the arms; ca.: 3rd quarter of the 1800's. Courtesy of Magnolia Manor. No Price Available

Louis XV Revival light weight gilded wood CORNER CHAIR; carved beading, and fluted posts; caster gone at front. $410.00

Roundarm LOWBACK CHAIR, 2nd French influence; gilded basewood; pierced splat and crest carvings, these first favored as bedroom pieces, then appearing in parlors and drawing rooms. $550.00

Stained maple JENNY LIND CORNER CHAIR;
these also desk or sidechairs; true spool turnings;
H. 38" at posts; W. 28".$650.00 – 750.00

Late century CORNER CHAIR in walnut with seat a rounded 90 deg.
of a circle – a quadrant – and mother of pearl armtop inlays; incisings;
casters; restored tapestry over coiled springs; seat is only 12"–14" from
floor; H. 30". $275.00 – 300.00

Mahogany CORNER (ROUNDABOUT) CHAIR, itself
a reproduction about 1875 as a Colonial Revival bor-
rowed from Chippendale with Victorian innovations;
original patterned velvet over coil springs; three claw
and ball feet; H. 32"; W. 23". $900.00 – 1,100.00

Mahogany CORNER CHAIR;
seats of strong cheaper woods
were often stained and veneered to
the basewood; here veneer over a
hard pine seat has slightly buck-
led; three turned legs with casters;
one cabriole leg with slipper foot;
(cabriole from the Chinese was
used in various American periods,
then revived in Victoriana during
the French influences of both
Louis XV and Louis XVI) H. 32";
W. 23½" ; D. 22". $450.00 –
700.00

Rocking Chairs

Belter style pierced back walnut ROCKING CHAIR, Louis XV Revival; scrollend arms, knee carved cabriole legs with whorl feet; H. 50"; W. 24½"; D. 25". During the late 1700's and early 1800's rockers were simply added to stationary chairs, then they became popular enough for chairmakers to include them as integral parts of original designs. $3,500.00 – 4,000.00

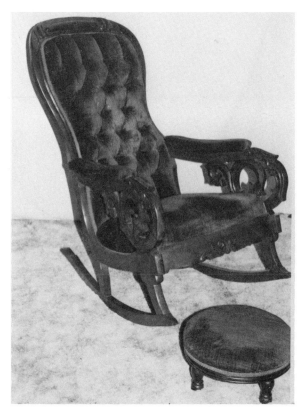

Black walnut ROCKING CHAIR with original red velvet; Rococo substyle, molded scrolls; known as a Lincoln Rocker – the style in which the President was sitting at Ford's Theatre; H. 43"; W. 24"; D. 39"; ca.: 1840 – 60's. $475.00 – 550.00. STOOL: $195.00.

ROCKING CHAIR; gondola curves (as a Venetian boat) comfortably padded; sometimes "Sleepy Hollow;" original tapestry; walnut frame with carvings; ca.: 1850 – 70's; a style having many midwestern makers; H. 42½"; W. 22½"; D. 38". $495.00 – 650.00

Oval back gondola curved maple lolling ROCKING CHAIR; eye caning; bentwood scrolls; finials; ca.: 1850 – 70's; H. 42"; W. 21"; D. 21½". $375.00+

Curly maple ROCKING CHAIR; Rococo influenced; carved oval top and scrolled demi arms; comfortably accommodates and bustle backs of ladies or acts as a Nursing Chair so when baby was laid across a lap it's head did not bump side arms; H. 40"; W. 23"; D. 24". $350.00+

Full arm ROCKING CHAIR; Rococo influenced; curly maple; oval eye caned back fastened to seat with splayed braces; H. 40"; W. 24"; D. 24". $350.00+

103

Maple NURSING type ROCK-ING CHAIR; incisings; balusters and spindle turnings; H. 40"; W. 19½"; D. 19". $250.00 – 275.00

Oak with quarter cut sections end of the century factory ROCKING CHAIR; especially popular rurally; slat-back; H. 44". W. 23"; D. 24". $250.00 – 275.00.

Oak ROCKING CHAIR; ca.: last quarter of the century; applied carvings as leaf scrolls, gargoyles, and fretwork outlined carved lyre; eight turned back and five each side baluster spindles; medallion seat; H. 40"; W. 26½"; D. 22"; country-popular. $225.00 – 250.00

Pressed back ROCKING CHAIR in deeper stained oak; caning; seven baluster turned spindles; ca.: late 1800's; country style. $175.00

105

Walnut ROCKING CHAIR; stained original woven reeds seat and back; two inset embossed top rails divided by a carved bowknots band; burl, sausage turnings; ca.: 1870 – 80's; Nursing Chair style in Eastlake lines; H. 40"; W. 20"; D. 23". $275.00

Maple and hickory ROCKING CHAIR; in 1850 – 75 Massachusetts, H. Hankerson produced such and less expensive pieces in large quantities; wide bevel-edge arms; scallops and beading; all posts turned as well as two front stretchers; acorn finials; Eastlake influenced; H. 36"; W. 19½"; D. 20½". $275.00 – 300.00

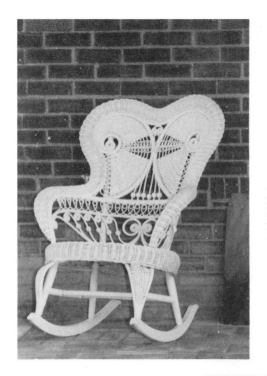

SPIDERWEB WICKER ROCKING CHAIR; hickory and maple white painted; small center upholstered seat; such elaborately reeded pieces were intended for indoors usage; also favored by photographers; H. 38"; Dia. 22½". $375.00 – 450.00

White painted WICKER ROCKING CHAIR with maple and hickory; button draped rolled-over seat continuing into arms and back uprights; peacock eye scrolls and fan splat — all designs bentwood framed; H. 38½"; seat at widest 25½"; D. 33½". $450.00 (Varies by region)

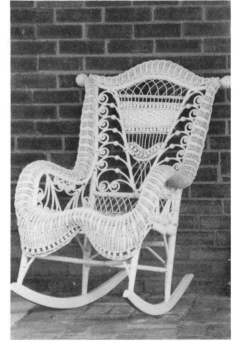

Rollfront white painted WICKER ROCKING CHAIR; maple and hickory; durably tight-woven; H. 40"; W. 20"; D. 21". $195.00

Deepstained WICKER PLAT-FORM ROCKER; ca.: last quarter of century; iron rail with locking device; chains draping two inverted thistle finials; H. 44"; W. 21"; D. 24". $650.00

Bentwood CHILD'S ROCK-ING CHAIR; six curved withes form seat and back, each fastened at front stretcher, top and seat frame back; white painted maple; used a cushion. $65.00 – 75.00

DOLL'S lightly woven white painted WICKER ROCKING and ARMCHAIRS; maple frames and hickory rockers. $125.00 Each.

CHILD'S white painted WICKER ROCKING CHAIR; maple caned seat and scrolls; maple framed WICKER ARMCHAIR; braided edges. $125.00 Each.

Black painted maple ROCKING CHAIR; ca.: 1870's; restored velvet; flat buttonturnings and finials; Eastlake style; H. 32"; W. 18"; D. 23". $95.00

FOLDING ROCKING CHAIR in walnut; ca.: 1875 – 80; original needlework; burl panels; carved crest; and spindles; H. 32"; W. 20"; D. 18". $125.00

Child's FIRESIDE FOLD-
ING ROCKING CHAIR;
original carpet seat and
back; hard maple. $110.00

Bentwood ROCKING CHAIR; black
painted light wood; braces; caned seat;
balloon curves. $135.00 – 150.00

CHILD'S ROCKING CHAIR; maple with tiger front legs; leather
seat center; caned back; gooseneck arms; paper underseat tag
dates: Nov. 10, 1860; H. 36"; W. 15½"; D. 15". $250.00 – 275.00

Curly and tiger maple CHILD'S ROCKING CHAIR; gooseneck arms; H. 36"; W. 15"; D. 14". $225.00 – 250.00

Deepstained ash CHILD'S ROCKING CHAIR; two carved splats; medallion reversed curved caned seat to accommodate continuous side uprights into legs; tulip crest carvings; wide deepcut apron; dated: 1873. $375.00 (Varies by region)

CHILD'S ROCKING CHAIR; stained hickory and maple; gooseneck arms; H. 28"; W. 14"; D. 16"; ca.: 1800's. $325.00

While being used, rocking chairs were prone to creep across a room. From the late 1860's non-creeping or Platform Rockers became popular, the chair's rockers engaged to flattened surface rails, becoming part of the whole with leather thongs, bracing, and/or springs.

PLATFORM ROCKER, cherry with china casters; original rose needlepoint; H. 38"; W. 20"; D. 24". $325.00

All original cherry dyed black PLATFORM ROCKER; springs; ca.: 1870; turnings; H. 39"; W. 21"; D. 27". $350.00

Slope back PLAT-
FORM ROCKER;
incisings; carved and
spindled crest; finials;
walnut with leather
upholstering; H. 42";
W. 23"; D. 28".
$350.00 – 425.00

Dyed hickory with original
tapestry upholstering;
ADJUSTABLE PLAT-
FORM ROCKER; H. 40";
W. 22"; D. 29½". $350.00 –
425.00

High Chairs

PULLUP HIGHCHAIR; Eastlake style with incisings; woven reeds; slightly splayed front legs add grace and strength from tipping; walnut; H. 38½"; W. 16"; D. 17". $300.00 – 325.00

'FIREHOUSE WINDSOR' PULLUP HIGH or YOUTH CHAIR; walnut with eye caning; stretcher; front legs; balusters turnings; H. 30"; W. 14 – 15"; ca.: 1870's. $275.00 – 325.00

PULLUP HIGHCHAIR with restrainer bar; wicker; repainted poplar; peacock eyes curls; narrow footrest; H. 40"; W. 14"; D. 14". $195.00

Uncommon solid-slatted back and seat PATENTED ADJUSTABLE HIGHCHAIR of deepstained oak; adjusts to low rocker; rest on wooden wheels for a toe-touch movement; can be set at medium height for play and easy feeding; curved ample footrest; wide rim food tray; H. 40"; W. 14"; D. 14". $450.00 – 475.00

Oak with caned seat HIGH-CHAIR; drops into low position; sausage turnings; an early piece; no tray; H. 38"; W. 14½"; D. 14½". $275.00 – 300.00

PATENTED ADJUSTABLE HIGHCHAIR; dark stained oak; caned seat and back wood framed; converts into low rocking chair confining child; rolls about on iron wheels; locks in three positions; H. 40"; W. 16"; D. 16". $400.00 – 425.00

Dining Chests, Servers, Sideboards

A touch of British royal elegance is this circa 1890 SILVER CHEST once belonging to the Dowager Countess of Carnavon, stepmother of the Earl of Carnavon, (whose fame relates to excavating the Egyptian King Tutankamen's tomb) having a brass plate engraved with her Berkley Square address in London. The Chest, soft fabric lined wood with iron straphinge and wide studded reinforcements, held precious silver table and serving pieces, perhaps kept in the butler's pantry for easily available cleaning and usage, also instantly ready for transportation to others of the Family's estates, a practice that extended to economically-able Americans. A Victorian's heart is said to have been very close to his stomach. He did enjoy his victuals! And both the diner and the servant or waiter needed trained familiarity with the proper application of each piece in the really appalling array of flatware laid at each table setting. $1,350.00+

During the 15th century a sideboard was a series of steps covered with gold or linen type cloth, standing against the wall of a room to hold plates and pottery wares. The late 1700's saw flat top side boards so long they had to be supported with eight feet. On these at either end tall wooden urns held flat silver tableware (the urns so difficult to handcarve that few were made here, most in England). Victorians shortened the extreme length of sideboards, going up instead of out. Corniced or fussily pedimented highboards towered over level surfaces, loaded with shelves, spindled rails, reeded columns, small mirrors that grew into big ones, and effusive incisings and basewood but more often applied, carvings. On southern plantations locked door and drawer compartments were used for security, known as SIDEBOARD SAFES or HOUSE SAFES.

Deeply carved and furred lions' feet that accent the four-door front of a cherry and burl veneer DINING SERVER (SIDEBOARD) 60" long; 48" high; 24" deep; Empire revival. $2,800.00+

Walnut and matched crotch veneer SERVER; two end columns on ball feet; L. 60"; H. 48"; D. 23". $1,800.00

Walnut and burl veneers SERVER; variegated sienna marble top; five brass pull drawers; caters; L. 62"; H. 36"; D. 24"; Eastlake manner. $1,200.00

SERVER with Empire elements; marble top; rosewood and burl; front-rounded side panels; L. 60"; H. 38"; D. 24". Courtesy Magnolia Manor. No Price Available.

Combined walnut and burl SERVER with carved fruit grips; Renaissance feeling with projection stiles; tassels; roundels; incisings; L. 60"; H. 38½"; D. 22". $1,200.00

Renaissance influenced SIDEBOARD; walnut with burl veneers; broken molded pediment; pierced cut crest; wide marble and two narrow wood shelves; H. 6' 6"; W. 48"; D. 24". $2,600.00+

SIDEBOARD; walnut with carvings framing oval door centers; original mirror; marble top and fretwork S-scrolls with 3 wood shelves; top could be used as candle rests; H. 7'6"; W. 40"; D. 24". $1,600.00 – 1,900.00

Victorian factory interpretations of 2 oak, partially quarter cut, 7' high, SIDEBOARDS. The wider 60" high, stained darker, has full Ionic columns, medallion framed mirror, incisings, applied carvings, and bracketed lions' feet. $1,200.00

SOLD...$975 in 1981. The other, 50" wide, in golden finish with bowed drawers, scrolls, and, as the other piece, Empire lions' feet, these largely emphasized; sold...$895; both ca.: last quarter of the century. $1,200.00

Empire substyle WINE CABINET; mahogany with burl veneers; glass knob on bowed drawer; carved-top columns and furred-top front feet; plain ball rear turnings; casters; H. 38"; W. 24"; D. 17½". Courtesy Magnolia Manor. No Price Available.

Bowed front Empire substyle cherry with paired crotch and burl veneer WINE CABINET; ca.: 1820-40's; turned columns; a rarity in design; L. 60"; H. 38"; D. 24". $1,500.00+ (Varies by region)

Dressing...Chests, Drawers

BACHELOR'S CHEST; mahogany with burl veneers and gilt; incisings; brass fixtures; metal flowers at a carved warbonnet frame having an inside burl ring around a beveled mirror; front-four-recessed drawers; projection stiles; secret recess behind pullout base panel; ca.: 1850's; H. 7'; W. 40". $2,500.00 – 2,800.00

DROPFRONT DRESSER, walnut; fruit grips on burl applied panels; candlerest shelves; tilting mirror; marble shelf; Renaissance broken molded pediment; H.7'; W. 40". $900.00+

DRESSER (chest of drawers with attached mirror); black walnut; fancy collared brass ring pulls; crested pediment; Renaissance substyle; H.7½"; W. 40". $975.00+

WISHBONE DRESSER; so called from the shape of the tilting mirror support; black walnut with crotch veneer; beading; handcarved pulls; marble shelf; ca.: 1870's; H. 6'10"; W. 36". $1,600.00 – 1,750.00

DROPFRONT cased DRESSER; combined walnut and burl; marble shelf; carpenter's lace around mirror; handcarved drawer pulls; split button turnings; incised and embossed handkerchief drawers; ca.: 1870– 80's; H. 6½'; W. 44". $1,450.00 – 1,500.00

DRESSER; butternut with handcarved fruit grips;
fretwork; marble shelf; liftop handkerchief boxes; concealed (secret) drawer at base slightly pulled out to display; Renaissance Revival; H. 7'; W. 42". $1,500.00 –
1,700.00

The painstaking simplicity of a rural maker in this deep-stained pine child's DRESSER with dovetailed drawers is interestingly combined with a sophisticated Rococo type embossed and gilded papier mache tilting mirror; then using what was at hand, the back is the unfinished wood sides of a shipping crate dated 1890, still readably stamped: INSTANT LOUSE KILLER, and showing a small girl period-dressed, dousing a chicken in one hand with powder from a can held in the other; H. 42"; W. 24". $375.00 – 425.00

GENTLEMAN'S CABINET;
mahogany; embossed deepset
door center; tilting original
mirror held by reeded posts;
brass and wood pulls; H. 7';
W. 21". $725.00 – 850.00

LADY'S CABINET in walnut and
burl (for bonnets and gloves);
could have been special ordered
for a particular space with door
opening on the right side; H. 5½';
W. 20". $595.00 – 695.00

Second French influences on a handcarved leaf and scroll surrounded image atop a low walnut CORNER CABINET for china and/or curios with a bowed glass door and three interior shelves; H. 5'6"; W. 30". $975.00+

CORNER HANGING CABINET (to be installed) with uncommon bowed front; carved walnut; no pull, opens only with a key; inside shelves; H. 36"; W. 24". $875.00

Rare BARBER'S CABINET; walnut with burl; spindled gallery; 2 of the 5 drawers lock; fancy brass; H. 6'; W. 30". $1,200.00+ per pair

Original false-grained wood on mustard yellow paint with applied panels and china knobs., Cottage type CABINET; 12 drawers numbered, inside pressed paper cubicles, actual usage unknown, dates around 3rd quarter of century...might've been in a quality Hat/Dressmaker's Shop. Probably 1 of a kind...$600.00+

Hall Furniture

Traditionally HALL CHAIRS were solid wood so cherished upholsterings would not be spoiled by wet clothing of messengers and servants. Prices range from $400.00 – 450.00; low averages are variable into the high hundreds. These pieces are well worth searching out.

One of a pair of HALL CHAIRS in walnut and burl; uncommon pullout drawer rather than liftop; Renaissance Revival; ornate with huge split incised glued on buttons; tall eared-urn at finial and smaller ones topping stiles; finger molded broken pediment; poplar inside drawer is secondary American wood; H. 50"; W. 22". $950.00 – 1,200.00 per pair

Gothic Revival oak HALL
CHAIR in golden finish; original
red velvet fabric; H. 54"; W.
22½" ; D. 24½". $475.00+

Gothic Revival HALL CHAIR
in black walnut with original
horsehair; split over a a coil in
the springs; fleur de lis points
and crest; inconspicuous brac-
ers on outside of seat frame
and back uprights. H. 40"; W.
20"; D. 22". Courtesy Magnolia
Manor. No Price Available.

Empire influenced walnut and burl HALL CHAIR; applied shield below a bonnet shell crested top flanked by ebon-eyed dolphins; paw feet; usually such a narrow liftop space held books and papers; H. 48"; W. 22"; D. 20". Courtesy Magnolia Manor. No Price Available.

Gothic-Renaissance Revival influences in black walnut and burl HALL CHAIR; slight brac-ers join stiles and seat at back of liftop hinges; large finial breaks deeply grooved pediment; H. 48"; W. 22"; D. 19". Courtesy Magnolia Manor. No Price Available.

Walnut and burl HALL STAND; marble shelf over glove drawer; iron drip pans and umbrella rests; 8 garment pegs; Renaissance Revival; H. 7½'; W. 36". $1,850.00

Plain and quarter cut oak HALL STAND; lift top overshoes storage makes a flat seat for putting them on; applied crest; four iron hooks; stained slightly darker than golden; H. 7½'; W. 40". $975.00 – 1,150.00

Rosewood HALL TREE; iron pans, marble shelf over glove drawer; six turned pegs; ca.: 1870; Renaissance substyle; held umbrellas, canes, and parasols; H. 7'. Courtesy Magnolia Manor. No Price Available.

Walnut HALL TREE; iron pan; molded bonnet top; H.7½'. Priced $750.00 but considering embellishments, range into the high hundreds and more.

Walnut HANGING HALL RACK with small shelf; original mirror; wood lace; molded pediment; turned garment legs; H. 30"; W. 22". $450.00 – 525.00

HALL SEAT CABINET in walnut; cup turned legs; lift top cover deep storage unit for papers, magazines, overshoes, and/or slippers; H. 18"; W. 24". $300.00 – 425.00.

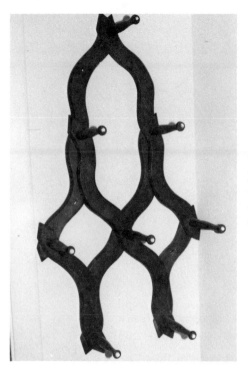

Walnut folding HAT & COAT RACK; china tips on turned wood pins; typical of a secondary rather than a formal entry. $175.00 – 225.00

Another informal entry CLOTHING RACK; bentwood hickory with generous knobends. $150.00 – 195.00

Ornate cast iron HALL
TREE; ca.: mid-century
Rococo substyle; leaf and vine
scrolls heart-frame the open
center; umbrella holds over
foliated drip pans; side hat
holders; H. 7'. $1,200.00+

One of the many popular miscellaneous novelties in cast iron,
UMBRELLA STAND embossed THE
REAPER; beading framed pan;
draperies, scrolls, florals and a sheaf
of grain over a shoulder; all original;
H. 30"; W. 17". $1,200.00+

Walnut UMBRELLA STAND; embossed iron pan; turned posts and molded edges; H. 30"; W. 14". $225.00

Black walnut UMBRELLA STAND; a rarity since cast iron is more often seen; shell design pan; Rococo substyle; fretwork; H. 36½"; Dia. 12". $295.00+

Mirrors, Screens

Bonnet curved mahogany MIRROR; applied carved fruit and leaves; finger molded frame; original glass; mid-century; H. 48"; W. 26". $350.00

Combined walnut and burl PIER GLASS; late century Renaissance adaptation; marble shelf; bird's heads on crest; H. 9'; W. 28". Found in Rococo Revival, especially when finished in burnished gilt tones, these are much more expensive. $1,200.00+

PIER GLASS, burnished gilt wood, marble shelf, Rococo Revival; applied carvings in the eagle above mirror, fruits, flowers, and shell patterns; H. 9'; W. 29". Courtesy Magnolia Manor. No Price Available.

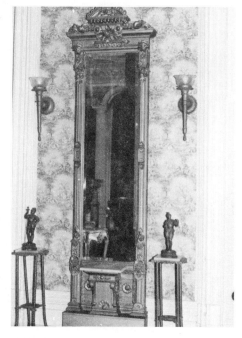

CHEVAL GLASS; ca.: mid century; for full length reflection in swinging original mirror; walnut and burl; gold leaf inlays; an opera hat tossed over side brass candle bracket, parasol leans below; H. 6½'; W. 36". $975.00+

FOYER MIRROR; ornately embellished butternut; beading; Classical Greek scrolltop, fluted and carved columns support the entabulature (cornice); recessed glass affords shelf; H. 8'; W. 60". $3,500.00

SCREEN, called by the owner "a southern piece" since the 1840–50's family possession is comprised of oak; fretwork carved and incised; applied ebony lion's head at center of wood lace crest; turned posts and rope stretcher; iridescent beads on cloth; entirely original. At each side a panel is knob-pulled out to 26" extensions; top pulls up to same height of center panel; picture is a uniformed figure on a prancing horse; folded H. 58"; closed W. 28". $1,800.00

Chinese influence FLOOR SCREEN; full carved cherry frame, hand-painted silk panels; folds flat; H. 72"; W. 18". $595.00+

Folding spindled walnut SCREEN; ca.: 1865; silk restored; center panel H. 5½'; W. 18"; each side panel H. 4½'; W. 24". $475.00

Walnut adjustable frame; original tapestried FLOOR
SCREEN; prevented glare from the windows and the fire-
place while seated nearby; H. 40"; W. 30". $250.00+

Music Boxes, Organs, Pianos, Stools

Victorians like home music, particularly MUSIC BOXES covering a whole gamut of styles and prices. Regina Models were popular. Automatic cylinder changers permitted playing several to a dozen records in turn. Their tinkling tones were fairly uniform with cost differences being in the cabinets. The Swiss were noted for fine "works," although German lines were and American lines later became quite excellent. Pump organs and pianos appropriate to our present room sizes are growing in demand, and their prices were not so variable as the Music Boxes ranging from $500.00 to $5,000.00 – 7,000.00 and more.

Handle cranked MUSIC BOX; walnut with crotch sides and trims; Regina Model, can be locked; uses perforated steel disk records; H. 54". No Price Available.

MUSIC BOX; embossed oak case; porcelain inlay design of children at play; The Criterion Model; plays approx. 16" steel records; closed H. 9"; L. 20"; D. 17½". No Price Available.

AMERICAN or CABINET ORGANS were favored in the late 1800's, producing tones when foot pedal pumped by the vibration of various shaped and sized reeds, also called REED or PUMP ORGANS.

PUMP ORGAN; cherry with applied burl; ecclesiastical Gothic influenced spires; fretwork and finials; carpeted pedals; gilded ebonized knob control panel; 'Nonpareil, L.C. Clark & Co., Worcester, Mass.;' mint operable; H. 6'; W. 4'; D. 30". $2,500.00+

Black walnut ORGAN with spindled gallery; candle/trifles shelves; H. 7'; W. 44"; D. 20". ORGAN STOOL adjustable with original velvet. Courtesy Magnolia Manor. No Price Available.

Walnut ORGAN; deeply incised and carved, turnings; cutout metal lyres over red plush covered pedals and lighter background fretwork at keys panel; H. 6'7"; W. 44"; D. 22½"; $2,600.00 (Varies by region)

PARISIAN BAND PIANOS, the ancestors of our Juke Boxes, were imported from France and were greatly enjoyed by Victorians at public amusement parks everywhere and in some music halls. Chestnut case; coin operated; spring driven; ca.: 1850. The top front, wood framed separate silk screen panels of hand designed swans, trees, and roses is removed to show how it operates. Keys striking 36-note piano wires, cymbals, drum wood block tambourine, and mandolin attachment bar are all activated, playing in unison with the revolving perforated drum L. 30", Dia. 12" which produced 10 successive tunes; fixtures are brass. Impressed on the solid panel is the company's name at 2 Rue Charles Baudelaire, Paris. $7,000.00

GRAND PIANO; Cable Co.; mahogany; heavy Renaissance style trumpet legs; ca.: last of the century, this 1905. $6,000.00 (Varies by region)

Ebony ORGAN STOOL; original cushion; Empire substyle; wide iron grips at each side of balusters level activate concealed rollers that raise and lower to desired height; H. 20"; L. 20"; W. 14½". $275.00

Adjustable ORGAN STOOL; maple pedestal; iron feet; original fabric. $450.00

Eastlake lines; ca.: 1870's; Maple ORGAN STOOL, original velvet; iron adjustable post. $200.00 – 225.00

Cherry ORGAN STOOL; original tapestry over coil springs; adjustable; ca.: 1850. $350.00

Ebony PIANO STOOL; fretwork; original patterned velvet; cutout demi arms; adjustable.
Courtesy Magnolia Manor. No Price Available.

Ebony PIANO STOOL; Empire influence; original cushion on coil springs; adjustable. $295.00+

Late century PIANO CHAIR;
pine; hard maple adjustable
seat; brass claws on glass balls
feet. $225.00 – 250.00

Walnut PIANO CHAIR; brass
on glass feet; glued on designs;
deeply grooved legs and post.
$225.00 – 250.00

Most abundant style to find PIANO STOOL in
maple; turns and adjusts to height. $175.00

Dark stained maple PIANO STOOL; turnings;
grooving; claw and ball feet. $175.00

Renaissance Revival combined cherry with walnut burl
MUSIC CABINET; heavy incisings; musical symbols;
drop compartments held with brass chains; H. 4'; W.
30"; D. 20". $750.00+

MUSIC CABINET; walnut and burl FALLFRONT; lyre center carved applied panel; glued on ebonized split buttons; gallery fretwork; H. 5'; W. 28"; D. 18". $850.00+

Cherry MUSIC STAND; the word MUSIC jigsaw cut on each side; brass chains for sides that open. $225.00 (Varies by region)

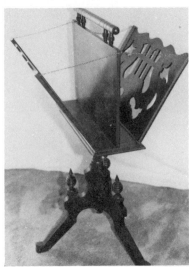

MUSIC STAND; walnut; fretwork lyre; carrying handle; brass chains hold sides. $275.00

Ottomans, Stools

Ottomans are overstuffed footstools, an extra (parlor) seat in use just prior to Victoriana and remaining popular throughout. Liking variety in stools, Victorians had low footrests, chair heights, and lift tops for slippers in hidden wells. With few exceptions all were factory made in assorted woods, some later redone in home needlework.

OTTOMAN; Empire substyle; mahogany; crotch veneers; original needlepoint conceals coil springs; H. 17"; 19" square. $250.00

In the fastidious elegance of Louis XVI is this Revival ebony
FOOTSTOOL; deeply gilded incisings; cushioned-hoof feet;
wings; and original fine damask; curule or 'Grecian Cross' legs;
mid-century — 1870's; H. 19½"; L. 18". $300.00 – 325.00

Walnut FOOTSTOOL; original velvet; these curved lines
easily and inexpensively made; resulting in Victorian
moderate prices. H. 20½"; L. 18". $225.00

Walnut FOOTSTOOL; Rococo Revival; original gold velvet over coil springs; serpentine legs; H. 16"; L. 18" W. 16". $250.00

Walnut FOOTSTOOL; iron casters; original fabric; H. 17"; L. 17½"; W. 17". $225.00

Walnut FOOTSTOOL; Renaissance substyle legs; casters; original silk; H. 18"; L. 18½". $225.00

Walnut and burl veneer BEDSTOOL; original tapestry; top lifts off for chamberpot storage; lower step pulls out for easier climbing into a high bedstead; H. 21". $325.00 – 350.00

Uncommonly ornate black walnut SLIPPERSTOOL;
pierced sides with carved front and rear stretcher crests that
touch the grooved collar framing original monkey and jungle
cat needlework with a velvet border; lifttop storage. H. 20";
L. 18½". $375.00

Combined walnut and burl carved SLIPPERSTOOL
turned to show brass hinges; skirted both sides for center
room usage; Eastlake style; original velvet; H. 18"; L. 19".
$375.00

All brass FOOTSTOOL; ebonied contrast; ca. : 1880; original tapestry with a bead-edged frame. $275.00+

Wide collar mahogany framing original needlework of FOOT-STOOL; early century mushroom feet; 15" Dia. $175.00 – 195.00

PRIE DIEUX (KNEELING STOOL...PRAYER STOOL); walnut; ca. 1830 – 40; hand-carved Biblical theme; rich silk restored to original; turned front feet, plain rear. $850.00

Quartered oak KNEELING STOOL; mass produced late in century; original red velvet. $175.00

Racks, Shelves

Hanging Towel Racks average L. 26"-27", hold at least two linens, and function in most rooms and entries including summer kitchens.

Black walnut TOWEL RACK; handcarved bird on a branch; leaves concealing top corner joints. $225.00 – 250.00

Black walnut TOWEL RACK with tiles; original needlework; Renaissance substyle with carved wings and large finials. $225.00 – 245.00

All original walnut double bar RACK; Rococo cherub and applied carvings. $195.00 – 225.00

Black walnut double bar RACK; ebony cameo bust; all original. $275.00+

173

PLATERACK in oak with walnut sliced button-beaded edge and protector moldings; narrow top shelf. $175.00 – 195.00

Maple PIE COOLING RACK; shelves tilt for flat storage; also a tea or muffin stand. $150.00

Walnut BEDDING (QUILT) RACK; three top bars and two lower hold firm the fancy cutout sides; these hold the 'spreads' for storage or as taken off the beds when retiring to 'spare' them. (Now sought for bathroom towel bars). $275.00

Walnut Eclectic PICTURE EASEL; Eastlake borrowing from Renaissance and Gothic; embossings; spindles; carvings; incisings; back bracer floor to top; door below picture-rest shelf pulls out for music storage compartment inside; H. 80"; W. 22"; ca.: 1880 – 90. Transplanted from studios into parlors, exuberant Victorians often further draped a large framed picture hereon with a plush or velvet swags, even setting potted vines at the base and trailing the tendrils upwards in an 'artistic' manner. Courtesy Magnolia Manor. No Price Available.

TRIPOD PICTURE EASEL; bamboo; folds flat; H. 6'. Prices on these lightweight types vary at lower figures while those of conventional solid woods, ornately embellished, command considerably more. $125.00 – 150.00

TRIPOD PICTURE RACK; maple; H. 5½". $95.00

After demonstrations of the new simply operated treadle tool at the 1876 Philadelphia Centennial, a 'gingerbread jigsaw' craze swept the country.

Walnut STANDING or HANGING COMBCASE; lift top storage forms a shelf; for 'last minute primpers', on going out, or if someone knocked. $195.00+

Walnut HANGING or CHEST TOP COMBCASE; barrel roll hides storage area; side holders could store matches, flowers, or one grooming tool while using another. $195.00+

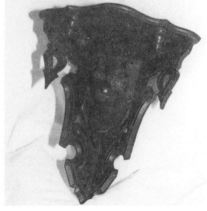

Wide walnut HANGING SHELF for various things as a small clock, vase, etc.; deeply incised. $150.00 (Varies by region)

Corner WALL SHELF; ebony, pendant-solid and fretwork-points; rare handcarved applied mastiff's head. $250.00+

Three jigsaw fretwork walnut
WALL SHELVES; all intricate
designs.

Carved tassels and chains.
Above: Wide surface and back.

Left: Delicate wood lace.

All $125.00 – 150.00.

Settees, Sofas, Couches, Divans

SETTEES (Lovers' Chairs, two people seats, Loveseats) average H. 36" – 40"; L. 36" – 44"; D. 22" – 24"; prices for fine quality originals in good condition ranging from $300 into lower thousands. SOFAS vary from demi length of 54" to the full 62" – 78"; H. 34" – 48"; D. 22" – 26", prices about $800 up. Circular DIVANS for 'cozy conversations', group usage pieces, comfortable seats in lobbies, home drawing, and smoking rooms, upholstered in plush, velvet, horsehair, or leather, might have the high backrest top in a flat or recessed wood round to hold a small potted fern or even a vase of cut flowers; prices were usually at a thousand and higher. All of this furniture was chiefly of coiled springs construction.

SETEE; red velvet on walnut frame; Eastlake style; mirror; carvings; incisings; and casters. $1,200.00+

Restored SETTEE; Eastlake lines; incisings, carvings, walnut. $850.00

Maple SETEE; peacock motif decorating medallion back; L. 38"; H. 36"; D. 28". Courtesy Magnolia Manor. No Price Available.

Demi SOFA; medallion back; Rococo substyle mahogany with gold velvet; puffy arms; serpentines. $1,200.00+

Demi SOFA; mahogany; horsehair; sleigh back curving from medallion center. Private Collection. No Price Available.

Walnut CHURCH SETEE – PEW – Renaissance influenced; applied carvings and moldings; burl insets; projection arm-rests; ca.: last quarter of the century. $395.00+

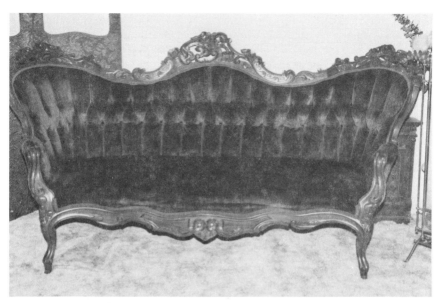

Rococo Revival SOFA; finger molded serpentine curves; pierced cut rosewood; ca.: 3rd quarter of the century; L. 74"; H. 38"; D. 33". $3,800.00

Full upholstered back tufted velvet SOFA; walnut; carvings; Rococo Revival; L. 60"; H. 36"; D. 30". $1,200.00

Gilded wood PARLOR SET, Louis XV Revival with a Grecian feeling in the Caryatids (draped figures portraying images of priestesses in the Temple of Diana used as columns supporting entabulatures); front cabriole legs with knee carvings and animal feet; SETEE H. 40"; L. 48"; D. 22"; GENTLE-MAN'S CHAIR H. 40"; W. 26"; D. 22"; LADY'S CHAIR H. 40"; W. 18"; D. 16"; casters only on front feet of each chair, on all 4 of the settee. Courtesy Magnolia Manor. No Price Available.

185

Rococo substyle SLEIGH BACK SOFA; mahogany serpentine lines; L. 72"; H. 38"; D. 26". $1,200.00+

Mahogany Rococo Revival SOFA; small flowered damask; among the most desired of the 19th century styles; L. 60"; H. 36"; D. 24"–26". $1,100.00

Renaissance Revival SOFA; rosewood with restored damask; bold carvings. $1,500.00+

Mahogany Empire Revival SOFA; restored silk; six supporting lions' paw feet, leaves, fruits, and nuts spewing from cornucopias above those at front; only a master craftsman could have achieved these carvings. L.78". $1,500.00+

Empire Revival SOFA (these with small variations known as 'Recamier' style, for a famed French beauty pained reclining on a similar Grecian-roll couch, which the artist himself designed for the painting); lions' feet and cornucopias of fruits and flowers; mahogany; L. 74"; one end 30" high; 22" high at the foot; D. 28". $1,600.00+

COUCH (LOUNGE); Turkish influence; patented concealed mechanism permits raising end into comfortable rests and lowering to an 8' daybed length; stained maple; L . 78"; H. 36"; D. 28". No Price Available.

Turkish influence CIRCULAR DIVAN (SOFA, OTTOMAN, COUCH); measures 6' diameter; ca.: 1880's; velvet; eight lions' feet in walnut on exposed narrow wood ring frame; (ribbons a museum protection). Secondary woods were normally used for the concealed base frames. Courtesy Magnolia Manor. No Price Available.

Two Louis XVI Revival Parlor Sets

Rosewood and burl veneers, three pcs.; eight-legged DOUBLE CHAIR-BACK SOFA with puffed out silk mirror oval wood framed; makes a comfortable seat for three people; L. 6'. GENTLEMAN'S CHAIR has wide curved arms, Grecian Caryatids at front; LADY'S SIDECHAIR without arms for more easily doing needlework and to accommodate hoopskirts; all have pendants; Grecian cameo heads on roundels of carved crests; chairs in various forms in sets. Courtesy Magnolia Manor. No Price Available.

191

Rosewood and burl veneers; cameo heads on roundels at carved crest are repeated on the SOFA and GENTLEMAN'S CHAIR at front arms; LADY'S SIDECHAIR has restored blending silk damask and is a one of a pair; this set has four pieces; sofa length 6'6". $2,800.00 – 3,500.00 per set.

193

Rococo substyle three pcs. PARLOR SET in walnut with original tapestry; button backs and arms; pierced carvings and serpentine lines. During the mid-century years masters were beginning to minimize frameworks with larger areas of bright upholsterings, this trend factory copied. 'Modern' SOFA is L. 58"; H. 42"; D. 26". $2,650.00+ per three piece set.

Matching GENTLEMAN'S ROCKING CHAIR is H. 46"; W. 26"; D. 20". The LADY'S ARM-CHAIR in exact pattern but in smaller dimensions was not available to photograph. (Such chairs are sometimes called HUSBAND & WIFE CHAIRS).

Sewing Machines

Maple cased SEWING MACHINE; mother of pearl inlays; brass bust of inventor Elias Howe, his name and 'Inventor & Maker, New York, U.S.A.' on a brass plate; lifting the sides lowers machine into well and brings top down for a work surface. Courtesy Magnolia Manor. No Price Available.

Cased walnut SEWING MACHINE; spiraled pilasters; saw-tooth trims; ornate brass pulls; foot treadle inside; doors open separately from a center post; on a brass plate; 'The Singer Machine, Trademark;' H. 30"; W. 33"; D. 22". $475.00+

Stands

STANDS, firm uprights to hold something, have been used for over 300 years, in Victoriana best relating to those primitive T-bar-foot essentials in purpose.

Walnut STAND with a projecting variegated chocolate/pink marble; handcarved mastiff with deeply cut clawmarks around the doghouse shelf upheld by a low center post; grooved pendants; four furred doglegs and feet in the Empire manner; H. 38" – 40". $750.00+

Walnut STAND; incised skirt is retaining collar for variegated chocolate/pink marble; handcarved twisted treetrunk and mastiff; deeper pawmarks on ledge; base post has three handcarved mastiff heads at top of three dog legs and feet; center opencut curls; H. 38" – 40". $750.00+

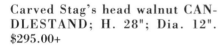

Carved Stag's head walnut CAN-DLESTAND; H. 28"; Dia. 12". $295.00+

Walnut CANDLE or LAMP STAND; in Victoriana these had slightly larger than earlier surfaces to accommodate lamps as well as candles; wood pinned and glued on Does' heads; H. 28"; Dia. 14". $295.00+

Walnut STAND with Eastlake scalloped aprons each side; finial pendants; bracket legs with bellflower finials; H. 30"; L. 18". $295.00

Mahogany STAND; inset marble; hoofed feet on legs mortised into pseudo pedestal; H. 32"; Dia. 18". $595.00

Walnut STAND; inset mother of pearl flowers with burl border inset in picture type frame; spindle held legs with burl cup finial center; H. 32"; Dia. 16". $400.00

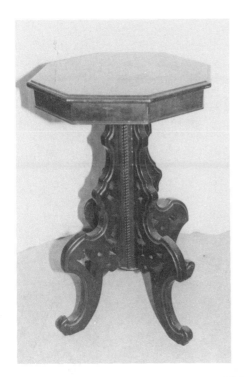

Hexagonal top walnut STAND; Renaissance substyle with split beads applied to post; fretwork; H. 32"; Top side to side 14". $375.00

Walnut STAND with applied base plaster composition embossing; ornate apron; spiraled post; brass animal's feet; top 20" square. $400.00

 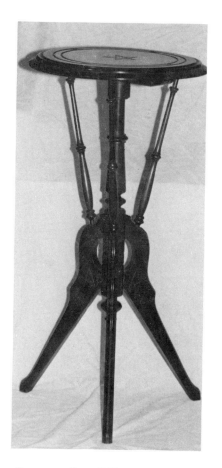

Mahogany STAND with carved pineapple; fluting and curves; H. 30"; Dia. 14". $395.00+

Customarily a BIBLE STAND in cherry; tripod style; five impressed top stars and groovings; ca.: late 1800's; H. 30"; Dia. 15". $250.00

Walnut CANDLESTAND,
button trims; H. 30"; top
dia. 9". $250.00

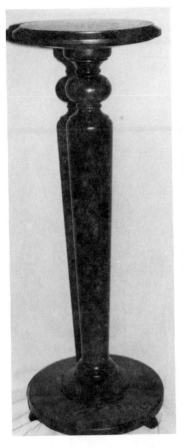

Dark stained oak FERN
/LAMP/CANDLESTAND;
heavily produced style; H.
40"; top dia. 11". $225.00

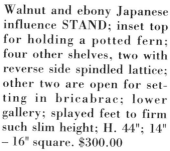

Walnut and ebony Japanese influence STAND; inset top for holding a potted fern; four other shelves, two with reverse side spindled lattice; other two are open for setting in bricabrac; lower gallery; splayed feet to firm such slim height; H. 44"; 14" – 16" square. $300.00

READING CANDLESTAND; revolving brass arm candleholder; walnut recessed surface; adjustable height roped iron pedestal; animal claw feet; H. 30" – 32"; Dia. 14". $300.00

205

Mahogany STAND; unusual; carved from one pc. of wood, twists have open division near top of post; rope edge at base of cornice-type overhanging surface; lions' heads bronze feet; overall distinctive embellishing; H. 34"; Dia. 18". $475.00

SEWING (or fern) STAND with Eastlake-Renaissance elements; original red and black painted panels with gilt outlines still definable; H. 28"; top L. 20". $225.00

Designed for the same purpose, two 'different' elaborate CANDLELAMP
STANDS have purely decorative bronze chains. The ebony one denotes
Egyptian influence with its bronze sphinx medallions applied to the collar of
of its marble top; Rococo Revival cabriole legs are carved, having deeply
gilded wing top scrolls and bronze tipped feet; its joiners are spindles while
the post base is a large ball pendant. No Price Available. The other STAND,
Rococo Revival influenced, has an onyx surface with castiron seahorses supporting its pseudo pedestal atop birds' legs and claw feet. $425.00. Both
pieces average H. 32" – 34"; Top Dia. 10" – 12". Courtesy Magnolia Manor.

Exotic Louis XV Revival LAMP STAND, ca.: 1850 – 60's; solid brass with a no-harm-crack in its 10" square marble; brass and onyx finials; profuse shells, leaves, and scrolls; H. 32" without finials. $600.00 (Varies by region)

SEWING STAND, wicker, bentwood, woven cane; 38" high; metal attached flowers; both supply baskets lidded; carrying handle; ca.: last quarter of the century. $210.00

Tables – Dining, Game, Parlor

Once a Table was a 'Borde' standing against a wall, placed for usage over sawbucks or trestles, whose expanded forms through the ages were legion. There were so many variations in Victoriana alone. The 3-a-day meals ranged from hours of formal elegancies to the grab and swallow at railroad passengers' brief pauses, this last leading first to the famous Fred Harvey's opening up our southwest travel in the last half of the 1800's with his chain of depot delicious-foods restaurants to the eventual rise of sumptuous dining cars on the trains. (In country kitchens leftovers were simply left on the tables after the noontime dinner until suppertime were handy for in-betweens and protected from flies with a cheesecloth held up the center by the tall vinegar cruet, whisked off at time to eat again.) Square Dining Tables average 60" – 64" closed, 30" – 32" high. Round Tables are about 48" – 54" in diameter, same height, and are now generally preferred. Most tables were made originally with one or more separate extension boards that fit with wood pins into precise joinings. Cost for both styles are about the same — $400.00 – 2,500.00 depending upon quality and markets.

A look of solid Jacobean substyle is in this square legged DINING TABLE with undertable support posts; heavily cut designs and unusual molded curved end stretchers; from an 1876 mansions' summer kitchen-dining room; 60" square; H. 30"; has one board in; made of butternut. Courtesy Magnolia Manor. No Price Available.

DINING TABLE; walnut; four spiraled posts with animal feet; curved stretchers; center two legs are held with a straight crosspiece in a moving pedestal one ·leg remaining stationary while the other swings to support any extra of four leaves; L. 72"; W. 60"; H. 30" – 32". Priced with six leather seat and back ˙straight chairs — one seen; Empire substyle. $2,200.00 (Varies by region)

Walnut DINING TABLE; five ponderously cut legs on casters assist two crested stretchers mortise-holding at each end and a curved scrolltop heavy support to carry the weight of the extra four leaves' extensions; decorated apron and Renaissance influences; 60" square closed; H. 32". $2,500.00+

DINING TABLE attributed to Grand Rapids manufacture; typical Renaissance Revival features; roundels and applied panels on molded legs; octagonal center post; solid table surface; no extra boards; H. 29"; Dia. 50". $1,500.00

Rosewood DINING TABLE; can comfortably seat 12 to 20 with its seven leaves; applied apron carvings; four legs; X stretcher with two turned post corners, one center column; molded brackets; Dia. 64" closed. Courtesy Magnolia Manor. No Price Available.

• Solid walnut DINING TABLE attributed to Berkey & Gay, Grand Rapids; ca.: 1860 – 75; octagonal split pedestal; four squared mortised legs with applied bracket scrolls and heavy cuttings; four leaves; H. 30"; Dia. 48". $1,600.00 (Varies by region)

Walnut GAME TABLE; Renaissance substyle; top lifts up and back to form a 38" long oval playing surface; short heavily turned pillar rests on a square block with large pendant finial; shaped and grooved angular sections with roundels mortised to the block from the legs and supports; H. 30"; ca.: mid-century. $1,200.00

212

Empire Revival GAME TABLE in mahogany; vase post and carvings at finial base; scroll feet platform; lifttop; H. 30"; L. 36". $675.00 – 750.00

Mahogany and burl lifttop GAME TABLE; lyre-shaped support on scroll feet base; H. 30"; L. 36". Joseph Meeks & Son, New York City cabinetmakers, advertised this type base on many of their Empire substyle tables. Courtesy Magnolia Manor. No Price Available.

Walnut GAME or TEA TILTTOP TABLE; baluster pillar with four attached shaped leg supports having Eastlake style applied brackets; H. 30"; Dia. 26". $675.00+

Painted and mother of pearl inlaid designs in this walnut GAME or TEA TABLE with its deeply cut leaves on the abruptly cutoff legs; tilting top; H. 30"; ovate 38". $1,200.00

Decorative Tilting Top TABLE of black painted PAPIER
MACHE having a wood column and iron feet; in the Oriental
manner; painted and mother of pearl inlaid scenic center oval
is surrounded by white, pink, and green florals in the same
iridescent shell inlays; wide molded table edge; Top is 26"x
23", Height as seen 42½"; ca.: 1850 – 60. $895.00+

Mid-century walnut GAME TABLE; 30" square, H. 30½";
ornately embellished with inlaid woods playing surface;
ornate brass pull drawers each side; apron spindles; galleried shelf; twists; beadings; incisings; and cushioned hoof
legs and feet; undertable X stretcher fastens at base of each
leg. $750.00+

Curious BIRDCAGE TABLE; the basic wood is hard maple; the top is inset keystone shaped segments with a plain round wood center and burl border; spindles hold the dropped rail; turned pillar has tripod scroll end legs with applied pierced cut metal trims; H. 30"; Dia. 28"; a late century novelty piece. $750.00 (Varies by region)

CENTER PARLOR TABLE; rosewood; chocolate marble cartouche; (turtle) top; bowknots on apron carvings; plumes at hips of cabriole legs with center finial surmounting shaped X stretcher; Louis XV substyle; H. 30"; ovate L. 38"; W. 26". $1,250.00

Marble top walnut center PARLOR TABLE; Rococo substyle; carved apron, cabriole hips, and stretcher; H. 30"; L. 30";W. 26". $950.00+

Oval PARLOR CENTER TABLE; walnut; white marble top; large crown finialed bracket curved legs on pillbox feet. Courtesy Magnolia Manor. No Price Available.

Renaissance substyle marble top walnut PARLOR CENTER TABLE; ca.: 1860's; legs mortised into octagonal posts; H. 32"; ovate L. 34". $975.00+

Walnut PARLOR CENTER TABLE; finger moldings; china casters; turned post and pendants; H. 30"; 32" oval. $895.00+

Variegated marble top PARLOR CENTER TABLE; walnut; Renaissance substyle; Dutch-cushioned feet; H. 28"; Dia. 30". $795.00+

Mahogany OCCASIONAL TABLE; Dutch cushion feet; H. 28"; Dia. 28". $295.00

Red leather partial top on PARLOR CENTER TABLE; H. 30"; Dia. 32". $325.00

Dainty OCCASIONAL TABLE in Rococo influenced mahogany; used elsewhere but mostly in bedrooms. $300.00

Walnut and burl PARLOR TABLE; Eastlake style; deeply incised wings below anchor hold the carved solid brackets of four square legs to the turned center post; ornate base; H. 30"; L. 30"; W. 20". $675.00 (Varies by region)

Walnut OCCASIONAL TABLE; variegated inset marble; bold finials; incisings; lighter inlays; H. 29"; L. 29½"; W. 18". $795.00

Mahogany OCCASIONAL TABLE; eight finial-pendants dropping from a piecrust edge surface; three legs' turnings match those of center pillar; H. 32". Courtesy Magnolia Manor. No Price Available.

Lightweight maple PARLOR TABLE; Cottage type; rope twists, button feet on turned splayed legs; drop rail held with corner balls, two between balancing the design; H. 32"; much favored for holding Stereopticon (handheld magic lantern type instrument for making double-view picture oblong cards into one-picture image) and its box of entertainment. $250.00 – 275.00

OCCASIONAL TABLE; sometimes a light work table; stained pine with spool turnings – low stretcher; ca.: 1870; H. 30"; L. 24"; drawer and shelf, Jenny Lind country type. $225.00 – 250.00

Plain and quarter cut stained oak TABLE; true spool and grooved turnings; beading; the claw-held balls are wood instead of more common glass; An underside original paper label carries: Matthews Bros. 1890...the other printing age-obliterated. $400.00

Roped edge maple TABLE; twists and X stretcher in Elizabethan influence; H. 32"; top square 22"; used a lot for family Bibles and plush covered picture albums. $400.00+

Only the legs and wood bead insets are not BIRDSEYE maple on this unusual TABLE; H. 32"; top square 22". $400.00 (Varies by region)

Empire Revival walnut and crotch TABLE; popular bedside style; richly carved four legs; brass mushrooms; H. 30"; W. 28". $750.00

Bowfront drawers on walnut and burl veneered TABLE; Empire substyle; only the top locks; H. 30"; W. 28"; D. 14". $600.00

Walnut and crotch veneer DROPLEAF TABLE; Empire
substyle; two drawers, top with S-roll front and under rim
finger slot pull; lower has ebonized knobs; H. 30"; closed
18"; Dia. 22". $750.00

Walnut Eastlake substyle; sawtooth skirt and galleried-shelf TABLE; H. 28"; W. 29". $300.00

In the manner of country Sheraton, a walnut with burl veneer TABLE liked for bedrooms and dining areas; copied by Grand Rapids and Buffalo, NY makers among others. $525.00

Walnut Empire substyle HALFROUND TABLE; popular side-wall foyer piece; tip of carved swan's wings, its neck, and the two of three legs support the top. $475.00+

Empire substyle SPEAKERS' LECTERN in walnut; carved storks on a burl oblong, their heads, in addition to a turned pillar, supporting a side-decorated and incurved rolled entabulature, the whole on a base embellished to match the surface; H. 40"; L. 20"–22"; from the hands of a skilled craftsman. $900.00

Mahogany CUTDOWN TABLE; urn shaped post with scrolled ears; carvings, groovings; H. 18"; L. 28". $295.00

Pink-chocolate marble inset top CUTDOWN TABLE; from original height to more-convenient desired useability; walnut and burl veneers; Renaissance Revival; elegant apron; H. 17"; L. 29"; W. 18". $400.00 (Varies by region)

CUTDOWN walnut and burl paneled TABLE; incisings; H. 17"; L. 30"; W. 20". $350.00 (Varies by region)

All original SALESMEN'S SAM-
PLES; mustard yellow paint on
poplar since that wood was
cheap and best lent itself to
being easily and attractively
painted; one an oblong oval the
other an aproned round, both
having cut-turned legs; Cottage
style. Above:$325.00 Left:
$395.00+

Wardrobes
(Armoires...large portable wardrobes, usually ornate)

Rare combination of cherry, walnut, and tiger maple
WARDROBE; peacock eye brass pulls; heavy overhanging cornice as seen on high quality furniture; H.
7'; W. 4'; D. 2'. $2,200.00

Ornately detailed oak and quarter cut ARMOIRE; borrowing from Rococo and Renaissance with shells, cornucopias, swags and bows, roped uprights, beveled glass doors and brass pulled three-drawers; H. 8'2"; W. 55"; all original. $2,500.00

Mahogany with crotch veneer WARDROBE...called
ARMOIRE in luxurious homes, particularly in the South
with emphasis on Louisiana; Rococo curves with a heavily
finger molded pediment and shell crest; ornate finials; brass
fixtures; handcarved woodgrips; H. 7½'; W. 48"; D. 20".
$2,400.00

Chestnut WARDROBE, fine-grained matched doors; brass pulls and hinges, the latter the only mechanical fasteners, for the entire piece is otherwise mortised together without any nails or glues, thus, easily taken apart to be moved; inside clothes pole; two lower drawers; H. 84"; W. 44"; D. 18". $1,750.00

Washstands, Commodes, Shaving Stands

Walnut and burl WASHSTAND; dovetailed drawers; circular cutout for washbowl; deep gallery to prevent splashing walls; ca.: 1840; Empire Revival; H. 34"; L. 26"; W. 18". $400.00

WASHSTAND; walnut and burl veneer; applied split spindles; ebonized teardrops; china casters; marble top, splashback, and candlerests; H. 36"; W. 28"; D. 18". $600.00

Empire Revival COMMODE in walnut and burl veneers; door compartment usually for chamberpot storage, although sometimes bowl and pitcher sets kept there; if a narrow strip of wood extends beyond the surface of the back, with or without empty screw holes, it means it was an original splashboard. Commodes differ from washstands in that they do have the chamberpot storage area. Pitcher sets were commonly kept on the outside shelf for display. $750.00

Empire substyle COMMODE in black walnut with projection roll top supporting a marble slab; two drawers to inside undivided area; note beading joints; ca.: 1845. Courtesy Magnolia Manor. No Price Available.

Empire substyle COMMODE; walnut; retractable bar one side golding towel; marble top and low splashback; carved fruit grips; ca.: 1845; these door compartments could hold water storage as well as toilet essentials; H. 34"; W. 30"; D. 18". Courtesy Magnolia Manor. No Price Available.

Walnut and burl veneers COMMODE; Eastlake style; pink-chocolate marble top and splashboard; ebonized and brass collared teardrop and knob pulls; H. 36"; W. 28"; D. 18". $475.00

Walnut and burl veneers COMMODE; brass bail and teardrop pulls; marble; H. 34"; W. 28"; D. 17½". $395.00 – 450.00

Tilting mirror with carved and molded crown, reeded columns COMMODE; walnut; dark variegated marble top and splashboard; brass two-drawer pulls and knob on door, other side held with an inside hook; S-bow top drawer. $450.00 – 475.00

Especially for country bedrooms, all-wood COMMODES and WASHSTANDS were adopted, even to the splashboards. It was easier to construct a drawer above two cupboard doors, sometimes with shelves behind one door without the extra work and expense of marble.

COMMODE; walnut and applied burl panels; front rounded corners; moldings; surface wear. W. 29"; H. 34"; D. 16". $400.00 – 450.00

Walnut COMMODE; teardrop pulls, candleshelves; moldings; bracket feet; W. 28"; H. 36"; D. 15½". $375.00 – 450.00

241

Eastlake style oak COMMODE; ca.: last quarter of the century; incisings; groovings; dull brass pulls; H. 34"; W. 26"; D. 18". $375.00

COMMODE in oak, sometimes known as 'Hotel Model'; Eastlake lines; high posts and rail held a splashcloth (often made of home embroidered washable cotton in 'turkey reds' on white),washcloths, or towels; incisings; towel bar extends about 22". $395.00 – 425.00

Tilting SHAVING GLASS; brass and mahogany; marble over a spindled square case with one drawer; turned pedestal on round base; ca.: 1860; H. 6'. $600.00 – 700.00

Japanese influence SHAVING CABINET; marble recess in shelf center for bowl; fretwork gallery; elaborate brass leaf fixtures; oriental embossings on lighter inlaid panels; storage space for shaving supplies and other linens; H. 6'; W. 28"; D. 18". Courtesy Magnolia Manor. No Price Available.

Whatnots, Etageres

Open shelves for holding bricabrac (small bibelots, trifles for remembrance), spindled Whatnots remain collectible in the original, still purchasable in the low to higher hundreds, albeit heavily reproduced; while Victorian versions of the elegant French Etageres (ornately sophisticated Whatnots) can vary from a thousand to several thousands and more, dependent on the area in which you shop — not plentiful in quality, however, at any sales centers...nor in quantity.

Rosewood ETAGERE; Louis XV, Renaissance, and late Classical influences; an approx. 7' tall combination of Belter type carvings; a slim pedestal supporting an urn shaped wood shelf; marble is white over the S-curved narrow drawer; detailed mirror framing; and Empire reminiscent rear feet with ball and button turnings at front; overall Eclectic. Courtesy Magnolia Manor. No Price Available.

Mahogany corner WHATNOT; molded edge and fretwork galleried shelves; graduated from base W. 16" to the top W. 11"; H. 6'. $375.00+

Flatwall WHATNOT in walnut; 12 carved, fretwork brackets hold the four corners of each shelf with whorled feet; wood lace galleries and a high crest that is scalloped below the shelf; H. 62"; W. 30" base; W. 14" top. $400.00 – 475.00

Flatwall WHATNOT; narrow shelves; walnut; true spool turnings at front, rear posts are plain rounds; H. 5½" ; W. 28". No Price Available.

Mahogany WHATNOT; graduated shelves with wood lace galleries (top and 4th shelf wearbroken) and molded edges; shelves separately supported by mushroom turned spindles; H. 5½'; W. from 16" to 24". Courtesy Magnolia Manor. No Price Available.

Glossary

ACANTHUS: Southern European plant's leaf design based in ancient architectural forms, renewed in Victorian carvings.

ANNULET: Small ring; decorative series of linked or separated rings or circles.

APRON: Skirt; plain or design-cut-edged wood strip at the base of seats, cabinet forms, and such; used as a trim or structural aid.

BAIL: Half-loop drawer pull or handle.

BELLFLOWER: Early used ornamental floral bud, carved or inlaid; 3 to 5 pointed petals.

BIBELOT: Small decorative novel or valuable cabinet object.

BUGLE BEAD: Tubular beads used on fancywork.

BULB: Elongated (extended) bulb form on such as chair or table leg stretchers.

BRACKET FOOT: Winglike or curvate sides triangular 'brace' or support for cased pieces.

BURL: Abnormal knotty outgrowth usually best quality on hard and semi-hardwood trees — walnut, mahogany, maple, ash — with mottled grain; thinly sliced, it was highly regarded as veneer for fine furniture.

CABRIOLE: Reversed-curve leg (bowlegged) used as early as the 1600's and reapplied in Victoriana; many variations in both legs and feet.

CASED: Enclosed; a place of security storage-sideboards, chests, cabinets, dressers.

CASTER: Small roller (wheel) set into foot or furniture base to facilitate moving.

CIRCA: About, around the time of; abbreviation ca.

CROTCH GRAIN: Wood for rich veneering cut from the V of a forked tree section; looks like ferns or flames; walnut and mahogany valued for their vein graining.

CYLINDER: As on secretaries, solid curved sliding top concealing writing surface and storage.

EBONIZE: To stain black to simulate ebony.

EMBOSS: Decorations raised (in relief) from a surface.

ENTABULATURE: A cornice, border, or platform; the topmost section of a column; all needing support.

ESCUTCHEON: A decorative plate around a keyhole.

FINGER ROLL: Continuing concave (hollowed out) rolls cut into the margins of a chair, settee, and so on.

FINIAL: A terminal piece, customarily ornate as urns, acorns, figurals, leaves, and so on.

GALLERY: A low fretwork or solid decorative and practical railing around the tops of furniture forms.

GIMP: Fancy narrow fabric trims

GINGERBREAD: Showy, excessive.

INCISE: Deep cutting surface designs.

INLAY: Decoratively setting contrasting materials into a recess, completion flush with the surface of the object.

LAMINATE: See page 17.

MORTISE & TENON: Method of joining two wood pieces by inserting one into the socket or mortise of the other; might also be further secured with a wood pin penetrating each.

PEDIMENT: Molded or otherwise ornamented structure topping a cased piece. **BROKEN PEDIMENT** is one interrupted with a separate crest at its highest point.

PENDANT: A decorative drooping element. **A FINIAL PENDANT** is a finial in reverse.

REEDING: Semi-circular straight cuttings that look like conventional reeds; the opposite of **FLUTING**, which is grooved, curved sections as in columns.

ROUNDEL: Any round or circular ornament — a furniture term.

SERPENTINE: Sinuous, wavy curves, usually with a convex center.

SPLAT: Center vertical piece in a chair back.

STILE: Upright element in a frame; the side supports of a chair back.

STAYRAIL: Horizontal crosspiece in a chair back for instance, firming the frame, often decorative.

STRETCHER: Horizontal underbracings as for chairs and tables, also once serving as foot rests.

VENEER: Thin layer of wood or various other materials glued to the surface of solid ground for ornamentation.

WHORL FOOT: Upturned scroll, a Knurl.

Index

OTHER BOOKS
BY
KATHRYN MCNERNEY

American Oak Furniture

American Oak Furniture, 2nd Edition

Antique Iron

Antique Tools: Our American Heritage

Kitchen Antiques, 1790–1940

Pine Furniture: Our American Heritage

Primitives: Our American Heritage

Primitives: Our American Heritage, Series II

Victorian Furniture: Our American Heritage, Book II

COLLECTOR BOOKS
A Division of Schroeder Publishing Co., Inc.

Schroeder's
ANTIQUES Price Guide

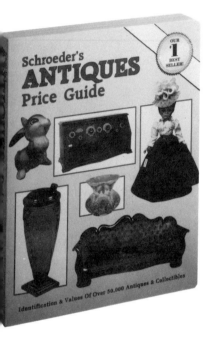

Schroeder's Antiques Price Guide is the #1 best-selling antiques & collectibles value guide on the market today, and here's why . . . More than 300 authors, well-known dealers, and top-notch collectors work together with our editors to bring you accurate information regarding pricing and identification. More than 45,000 items in almost 500 categories are listed along with hundreds of sharp original photos that illustrate not only the rare and unusual, but the common, popular collectibles as well. Each large close-up shot shows important details clearly. Every subject is represented with histories and background information, a feature not found in any of our competitors' publications. Our editors keep abreast of newly-developing trends, often adding several new categories a year as the need arises. If it merits the interest of today's collector, you'll find it in *Schroeder's*. And you can feel confident that the information we publish is up to date and accurate. Our advisors thoroughly check each category to spot inconsistencies, listings that may not be entirely reflective of market dealings, and lines too vague to be of merit. Only the best of the lot remains for publication. Without doubt, you'll find *Schroeder's Antiques Price Guide* the only one to buy for reliable information and values.

8½x 11", 608 Pages   **$12.95**

COLLECTOR BOOKS
A Division of Schroeder Publishing Co., Inc.